THE TWELVE TRADEMARKS OF GREAT LITERATURE:
A COLLECTION OF ESSAYS, STORIES AND POEMS

J.F. Baldwin

FISHERMEN PRESS

© 2002 by Jeff Baldwin and Fishermen Press
Worldview Academy
P.O. Box 310106
New Braunfels, TX 78131
(830) 620-5203
fishermenpress@hotmail.com

ISBN # 0-9720890-0-4

Cover design by Jeff Stoddard

To Emma:
We're praying that the day dawns and the
morning star rises in your heart (2 Peter 1:19)

CONTENTS

STORIES

ESSAYS

THE TWELVE TRADEMARKS OF
GREAT LITERATURE

Many Christians think that they have done their cultural duty when they turn off the TV, avoid steamy movies, and break their heavy metal CDs. They think the battle is won by *not* reading Harry Potter.

But Philippians 4:8 makes it clear that eschewing the bad isn't enough. Christians should also seek out the true, noble, right, pure, lovely, admirable, excellent and praiseworthy. As T.S. Eliot says, we have the "responsibility of patronage of the best that is made and written."[1]

This means, among other things, that Christians should read the great books—which would be pretty simple if it wasn't for that tricky little adjective. What makes a book "great"?

Not just popular opinion. A moment's glance at any bestseller list demonstrates this; no matter how many people think that *Atlas Shrugged* is a great book, it isn't. Believing something is true doesn't make it true.

Other worldviews may exalt the reader's subjective response, because these worldviews have rejected a fixed standard. But if Christianity is true, then the source and standard for the good, the true, and the beautiful is the character of God. *Your* attitude toward the book isn't the standard—*God's* attitude is. And the mature Christian isn't satisfied with his literary taste until it fully conforms to the taste of his Creator.

In one sense, then, the process of judging the "greatness" of a book is straightforward: we carefully consider the content of the work, formulate the theme, and then compare the theme to the biblical truth. If the theme is biblical, and the moral framework glorifies righteousness and discourages sinfulness, then the content of the book is great.

Unfortunately, great content doesn't guarantee that the book is great. Many people know truth, but *not everyone who knows truth can write.* And just as you wouldn't trust every trustworthy person to build your house—you'd want to know if that person was a skilled craftsman first—you also can't trust every trustworthy person to write a great book. Great books have more than great *content*—they have great *form*, as well.

Which creates a real problem. Judging the content of a book is not that daunting, because Christians know where to find the standard for content: God's Word. But where does one find the standard for form?

It would be nice if the standard for form was spelled out in God's Word—for example, I would certainly feel much safer judging the literary merit of a book if I could turn to the back of my Bible and find an appendix written by St. Paul that listed every great novel in history. But my Bible doesn't have that appendix, and I suspect neither does yours.

How, then, can a Christian know if a book is well-written or not? If we don't have the answers in scripture, are we stuck relying on our own fallible reason?

I don't think so. Romans 1:20 tells us that God has revealed Himself to men not only through the Bible but also through creation: "For since the creation of the world God's invisible qualities—his eternal power and divine nature—have been clearly seen, being understood from what has been made, so that men are without excuse." This general revelation provides Christians with many helpful clues about how aesthetics can reflect the character of God.

How can I be certain that God is concerned with beauty? I need look no farther than His creation. A grove of aspen trees clearly reveals that God values beauty. He says as much in Genesis 2:9: "And the Lord God made all kinds of trees grow out of the ground—trees that were pleasing to the eye."

What's more, these trees give me clues about elements of beauty. One obvious element of God's beautiful creation is *order*. This means that I should expect successful literary forms to be orderly. Not only will words combined at random be ugly, but also the more complex and fulfilling the ordering of language is, the more beautiful the book will be. This sort of "deep order" refers to elements like proportion, balance, symmetry, and rhythm.

Light, too, appears to be a crucial element. Light should reveal color, and darkness should reveal only shades of black. Books that manipulate light well manage contrast and movement well. They also reflect moral absolutes, understanding that although men may be drawn toward the dark, men are rarely so deceived as to mistake darkness for light.

This implies, then, that the person who says he doesn't know how to define art but "he knows it when he sees it" is not far from the truth. Just as every man recognizes the beauty of a sunset or of a deer bounding through the forest, every man recognizes man-made beauty when he sees it—at least, as long as that man-made beauty is so skillfully executed that it clearly reflects God's order and light. Put more simply, even people with little musical ability realize the beauty inherent in Handel's *Messiah*. In this sense the *Messiah* is as obvious as the Grand Tetons in January.

This would seem to solve our problem discerning which books are great. Does the beauty of the book strike you like a falling star? Then the book is great.

But this also seems to lead us right back to the problem

of subjectivity. What if one person considers a book beautiful and another does not? How can we know who is right and who is wrong?

To answer this, you must first notice that some books are considered beautiful by almost every thoughtful reader. Homer's *Odyssey*, Dickens's *Great Expectations*, Dostoyevsky's *Brothers Karamazov*—such works are so skillfully done that their beauty is self-evident.[2] These books fall in the "I know art when I see it" category; they align themselves so closely with God's created beauty that each reader's subjective response aligns itself with God's objective standard. The problem of discerning the beautiful only arises with lesser works.

But this indeed is a problem. What should we think, for example, of *Uncle Tom's Cabin*? Critics are fairly harsh with this novel, but the average reader is often awed by its beauty. One critic, John William Ward, states the problem this way: "For the literary critic, the problem is simply how a book so seemingly artless, so lacking in apparent literary talent, was not only an immediate success but has endured."[3]

Whom should we believe? Is the critic right, or the average reader? Is *Uncle Tom's Cabin* a great book?

Obviously, Christians who recognize the profundity of the book's content are more likely to call it "great." Setting *content* aside, though, is it possible to render judgment about the *form* of *Uncle Tom's Cabin*?

Yes and no. We can never achieve absolute certainty about the final quality of this book because we are fallible human beings. Even mature Christians err, especially in matters not directly decided by God's Word. This means, then, that our discussion of the artistic merits of literature must be characterized by humility. We must be ready to listen, and we must acknowledge that others may be more discerning than we are.

This does not mean, however, that the Christian reader is utterly adrift, unable to render any meaningful judgment at all. Thanks to God's general revelation in His creation, we can follow certain clues and draw reasonable conclusions. I may not know (until I get to heaven) whether or not *Uncle Tom's Cabin* is more beautifully written than *Moby Dick*, but I certainly know it is more beautifully written than the Hardy Boys. Humility need not give way to the meaningless modern "tolerance" that treats every assertion as equally valid.

With that in mind, then, this essay suggests twelve trademarks of great literature. I believe there are twelve elements that contribute to the excellence of the form of a book. These elements are:

1. The dogma is the drama.
2. Maintains proportion and perspective.
3. Maintains the appropriate pace.
4. Demonstrates an economy of words.
5. Flows uninterruptedly.
6. Unfailingly chooses the *mot juste.*
7. Makes the reader sympathize with at least one character.
8. Rewards attentive re-reading.
9. Shows rather than tells.
10. Expresses the inexpressible.
11. Moves you.
12. Creates with a distinct voice.

You'll notice that none of these "trademarks" are my own invention, and with the exception of the first, all of these trademarks have been generally accepted by critics throughout history. It should be this way. Beauty is not the property, nor the discovery, of one man. Many discerning men and women have worked to articulate what constitutes beauty. This essay simply seeks to distill that work into a manageable yardstick.

You should also bear in mind that great *form* is only half the battle. If the form of a book is great but the content is bad, the book may be artistic but it is not worthy of the Christian's contemplation and meditation.

Don't be surprised, though, to find that form and content are closely related. This is certainly true in the case of the first trademark.

The dogma is the drama

Dorothy Sayers, one of the greatest Christian thinkers of the 20th century, was the first person to clearly articulate this concept.[4] Sayers wrote terrific murder mysteries, and she understood that in her mysteries, the dogma provided the drama. That is, *the moral tension drives the plot.*

What happens in a murder mystery? Someone gets murdered—and at this point the reader experiences moral tension. The reader knows that murder is wrong, and so he or she hopes that the killer is discovered and brought to justice. The drama of the story is bound up in the *morality* of the story.

Although Sayers never claimed as much, I believe that the dogma is the drama in all works of great literature. In order to tell a great story, the author must make his reader care about the right outcome. And the way we cause someone to care is to appeal to his sense of right and wrong.

This has implications for both the *content* and the *form* of a novel, as Christian author and professor Edward Veith recognizes: "Just as morally bad books are usually aesthetically bad as well, good books—even those by non-Christians—are usually in accord with God's created order both morally and aesthetically."[5] I would say it a little more emphatically: the form of a book will suffer if the author forgets to rely on God's moral laws to create the tension in the story.

Suppose you were trying to write the great American novel—better than *East of Eden*, better even than *To Kill a Mockingbird*. Obviously, the audience for such a masterwork is incredibly diverse. Your novel would have to appeal to people from vastly different cultures, with vastly different worldviews, who may be young or old, male or female—who may not even be born for another couple of centuries!

How could you possibly write a book that appealed to such a diverse audience? How could you even be sure that every reader would be cheering for the same outcome?

How? The author must *play by the rules that are written on our hearts*. Romans 2:14-15 makes it clear that God grants every man a conscience, and that this conscience helps everyone to be certain about a few moral judgments—murder is wrong, bravery is preferable to cowardice, etc. Rules like these are universal—every man refers to them, even if not every man is willing to acknowledge their existence.[6]

The classic example of this, unfortunately, is provided by a movie instead of a book. I've heard many earnest Christians claim that the first *Star Wars* movie was biblical because it depicted "the battle between good and evil." These Christians acknowledge the obvious Taoist undertones in *Star Wars*, but dismiss them because the movie causes us to cheer for the brave and kind freedom-fighter, Luke Skywalker, against the cruel tyrant, Darth Vader. Because good triumphs over evil, the argument goes, *Star Wars* must articulate a Christian message.

Not exactly. *Star Wars* certainly assumes the truth of Christian morality to establish tension to drive the plot—but that doesn't mean the theme of the movie is Christian! George Lucas simply did what countless authors have done before

him: implicitly assume Christian morality to coax his readers
to cheer for the right things. George Lucas is not a Christian,
and he doesn't even embrace the idea of moral absolutes, but
*he has to rely on moral absolutes to ensure that his audience
is cheering for the right outcome.* Star Wars would not have
been such a smashing success—or a success at all—if half of
the audience cheered when the Death Star blew up, and the
other half wept.

This is how we know a tragedy is a tragedy. If you
didn't think it was *wrong* for Iago to deceive Othello and for
Othello to kill Desdemona, you wouldn't view Shakespeare's
play as a tragedy. But no one seriously asserts that *Othello* is a
comedy. We all *know,* thanks to our conscience, that tragedy is
tragedy.

Please notice that I am not arguing that every author of
every great book has to consciously embrace Christian ethics.
Clearly, many great authors—from Ernest Hemingway to
Albert Camus—would be horrified to hear that their works
rest on absolute morals grounded in the character of God.
Whether they like it or not, however, every atheist author and
indeed every author must implicitly assume the existence of
moral absolutes, even if they are simultaneously explicitly
denying them.

Why do you care about what happens in *The Old
Man and the Sea*? Not because you are sympathetic to
Hemingway's worldview; not even because of the sheer
beauty of the prose. You care what happens to Santiago
because Santiago demonstrates kindness and perseverance.
If he were a selfish quitter, you wouldn't finish reading the
book.

This example also suggests the test of this trademark.
If this trademark is valid, it should apply to almost every
acknowledged classic in history. If a number of great books
contradict this trademark, it's probably not legitimate.

Which brings me to *Robin Hood*. When I became aware of Sayers's statement that the dogma is the drama, I thought of this book rather quickly. It seemed obvious to me that *Robin Hood* contradicts Sayers's idea. Robin Hood's story clearly suggests that robbing the rich is justifiable, and this conclusion isn't in keeping with what our conscience tells us. *Robin Hood* apparently breaks the first trademark of great literature.

But does it? Yes, the act of robbery is immoral—but how does the storyteller manipulate us to ensure that we cheer for the robber Robin Hood?

The answer lies in the choices that the author extends to the reader. We may either cheer for a brave archer who is also loyal, kind, and merciful to the poor, or we may cheer for the Sheriff of Nottingham. Pretty easy choice, don't you think? We may not love everything that Robin Hood does—indeed, some of it may go directly against our conscience—but there is little doubt that, in the limited world of Sherwood Forest, our sympathy must be with Robin Hood and his Merry Men. The Sheriff commits gross injustices and these brave men are doing their level best to thwart that evil. We want to see them succeed. If Atticus Finch lived in Sherwood Forest he would provide an even more appealing choice for the reader, but he doesn't. Given the choices, everyone's conscience gravitates toward Robin Hood instead of the Sheriff.

It seems to me, then, that *Robin Hood* abides by this trademark. In fact, I have only been able to think of one "classic" that definitely contradicts this trademark: *The Three Musketeers*. Like all modern readers, I came to the story of *The Three Musketeers* knowing I was supposed to cheer for the title characters—so I was surprised to find that I had no desire at all to see the musketeers succeed. Whether they lived or died, won fame or lost in anonymity, was all the same to me. And I think the reason is clear: my conscience rebelled against the behavior of these "heroes." Each musketeer's central purpose, it seemed, was to fornicate. They set out on dangerous missions chiefly because they hoped to gain glory and thereby seduce other men's wives. Such a purpose is base, and renders all their bravery base. Alexandre Dumas did not persuade me, the reader, to cheer for the right people or the right outcome, and so his story failed.

Does this mean, then, that *The Three Musketeers* is not a great book? It is perhaps a measure of how important I believe this trademark to be that I would suggest such a conclusion. I believe that the popularity of *The Three Musketeers* has more to do with Hollywood than the power of Dumas's story. I may be wrong, of course—but if I am I do not think it is because Sayers was wrong about the dogma providing the drama. Perhaps instead, Dumas manages all the other aspects of his novel so well that he can overcome what I view to be a crucial flaw. In any case, *The Three Musketeers* is the only "classic" I have encountered that does not rely on moral tension to drive the plot.

And if indeed it is true that every great book plays by the rules written on men's hearts by God, then there are profound implications for the Christian studying literature. Suddenly every great book is another reminder of the "moral proof" for the existence of God—reminding us that universal laws strongly suggest the reality of a law-giving Creator. What's more, Christian students may use great literature to point out this truth to non-Christians.

Suppose, for example, that a college freshman who is a Christian finds herself enrolled in a secular course on American Literature, and the first book the class is assigned is *The Grapes of Wrath* by John Steinbeck. Absent the understanding that the dogma is the drama, that student would be faced with a purely defensive battle—trying to convince her professor and fellow students that this moving novel has a Marxist theme and that Marxism is a flawed worldview. A well-prepared Christian student could make some good points, but she would be fighting a battle far removed from the central questions about the nature of God and the nature of man.

On the other hand, a student who understands this trademark would read *The Grapes of Wrath* with an eye toward discovering the underlying moral assumptions that drive the plot. Once the student discovers this underlying moral framework, she could help her fellow students recognize Steinbeck's implicit assumption of moral absolutes. She might, for example, raise her hand and ask her professor why Steinbeck seems to assume that his readers would hope that his main characters wouldn't starve to death. Doesn't this imply an appeal to a moral absolute that decrees that life is sacred? And where on earth does Steinbeck find such an absolute, since he rejects the concept of a Creator?

Obviously, such a discussion of Steinbeck's work would prove much more fruitful for that student's classmates than would a discussion of Marxism. It might even be hoped that some students would face, perhaps for the first time, their own implicit assumptions about morality, and from whence those assumptions come!

Understanding that the dogma is the drama does *not* provide the reader with a "Christian method" for reading great books. Rather, it helps the Christian recognize and remember the moral laws that permeate our existence so thoroughly that we often take them for granted. Rather than providing a Christian method for reading, this trademark provides the only method for reading that is entirely cognizant of the universe in which we live. It reminds us that Christ is not just one religious leader among many but rather the Way, the Truth and the Life—the very source for all that is Good in the world, including mankind's understanding of the Good.

If this is true, then this first trademark is the most significant of the twelve trademarks. But books still must adhere to other trademarks to be considered "great."

Maintains appropriate proportion and perspective

This trademark simply refers to the fact that, as Louis Whitworth says, "Fiction has no limits in time or subject, but it should be faithful to its own framework in order to 'work.'"[7] That is, if something occurs in a book that is significant according to the framework of the book, it should be treated as significant.

Edith Wharton provides a terrific example of this in her nihilistic novel *Ethan Frome*. At one point in the story, a cat knocks a pickle-dish off a table, and the pickle-dish breaks. If this happened in your own life, you would probably not view it as a particularly significant event—but in the story of *Ethan Frome* it creates an immediate and dangerous crisis. When Wharton writes that "The case was so serious that it called forth all of Ethan's latent resolution,"[8] we believe her. She has helped us achieve the proper perspective regarding this sparse and frightening story.

This trademark also requires the author to maintain the proper perspective with regard to the trivial and the profound. If an author seriously elevated the trivial or denigrated the profound,[9] readers would find themselves disagreeing with the author's entire framework. For example, a serious novel based on the theme that a preference for chocolate ice cream over vanilla is an abomination would be ignored or ridiculed by the general public.

Conversely, if you were writing a novel that dealt with

the most profound things—heroism, life and death, and the battle between good and evil—you would do well to establish a robust framework that could contain such momentous concepts. J.R.R. Tolkien's trilogy *The Lord of the Rings* "works" partially because he doesn't attempt to describe a central moment in the conflict between good and evil in a short story or a novella.

Notice, too, that Wharton avoids the mistake of elevating the trivial. Although a broken pickle-dish is *usually* a trivial thing, in her story the pickle-dish alerts a wife to her husband's infidelity, which is most emphatically *not* a trivial thing.

Maintains appropriate pace

The third trademark of great literature is linked closely to the second. Just as great books should maintain appropriate proportion and perspective, they must also maintain the appropriate pace. "They can't yank a novelist like they can a pitcher," writes Hemingway. "A novelist has to go the full nine [innings], even if it kills him."[10] The author is free to compress time, flash back, flash forward, slow time down, make it stop—but only when it doesn't shatter the overall pace of the work. As unfair as it might sound, any manipulation of time is allowed in a book if it *works*. But any manipulation of time that confuses, bores, or offends a good reader is unacceptable. The author must persevere within his novel's established "fourth dimension" even if it—yikes—kills him.

In a work like *Pilgrim's Progress*, the importance of time-management is fairly obvious. The physical length of Christian's journey is determined, at least to some extent, by the time required for such a journey. If Christian's journey is too long and involved, then the story would take too long to tell. Likewise, if Bunyan equates Christian's journey with a very simple step like passing through a gate, then the story would drag if it were told for more than a few pages. Bunyan splits the difference nicely; although, to our modern ears, C.S. Lewis does a better job in *Pilgrim's Regress*.

Significantly, one of the greatest books ever written breaks this rule. Like *Pilgrim's Progress*, this story centers around a journey, and like *Pilgrim's Progress*, the journey is of manageable length. Still, *The Adventures of Huckleberry Finn* does not maintain the appropriate pace. As foolish as it seems to find fault with such a fantastic book, by Mark Twain's own account the story ultimately breaks down. According to Twain, he became impatient with his story around the time he introduces Tom Sawyer into the plot, and the rest of the book winds down too quickly and too neatly. The reader has the sense of a beautiful, measured conversation hastily ended because someone heard the phone ringing. To put things in Hemingway's terms, the pitcher gave up the game in the eighth inning.

It should be noted here that the public's standard for proper pacing has changed over the years. The leisurely pace of Jane Austen or Sir Walter Scott makes my modern students gnash their teeth. The fact that we have moved from a literary culture to a video culture, as Neil Postman points out, means that modern readers will tolerate little character development and less description. "Nothing happens" in a book, according to my students, unless the first chapter features at least two murders and a car chase.

This just means that moderns have a problem with perspective. Our idea of appropriate pacing is too narrow; it needs to be expanded to include subtle discussions and loving descriptions. But this does not mean that modern readers need to tolerate *inefficient* time management. Detours worth taking are allowed; foot-dragging is never acceptable.

Demonstrates an economy of words

One special type of foot-dragging is wordiness. Weak writers often fail to take the time to shave their prose—apparently assuming that if you throw a lot of words at an idea, some of them will stick. All of us have read works that use words indiscriminately, and all of us can identify these works as poorly written.

This is one element of the fourth trademark, but it is not the only one. Certainly, stories that use too many words don't demonstrate an economy of words. Wordy writers need to remember F. Scott Fitzgerald's admonition that "a writer wastes nothing"[11] and Twain's advice: "As to the adjective: When in doubt, strike it out."[12] But there is another way to mismanage word count.

See Spot run. On the opposite end of the spectrum from Ayn Rand's ramblings are books that are too *stingy* with words. It's true that there are a hundred spendthrifts for every miser with words, but ever since Hemingway some authors equate miserliness with skill.

Being economical with words should never degenerate to a paucity of description or information. Hemingway is only occasionally guilty of this; Franz Kafka, in my opinion, is often *too* sparse.[13] If you feel like you're reading a newspaper account or a children's story, it's quite possible that that author has broken this trademark by being too sparing with his words and meaning.

It is worth warning today's readers again that our perspective may be a bit skewed. Almost every modern reader, at least when he first meets Charles Dickens's books, secretly (or openly) curses him for his wordiness. I can still feel the intense relief that accompanied turning the last page of *Bleak House*, punctuated by throwing my cheap copy of that book off the roof of a four-story building. I remember thinking that the book had *almost* killed me, but that in the end I had killed it. And of course I vowed never to read Dickens again.

But Dickens almost always has the last laugh, and for good reason. His books are long, certainly, and he introduces far more characters than seems prudent—and sometimes he'll even reserve a whole paragraph to describe someone's eyelashes—but for all that, *Dickens doesn't waste words*. You may be frustrated by how much of his world Dickens wants to tell you about, but you may not complain about his management of words. Consider the following passage from *A Christmas Carol*, dedicated only to describing a large and gloomy staircase:

> You may talk vaguely about driving a coach and six up a good old flight of stairs, or through a bad young Act of Parliament; but I mean to say you might have got a hearse up that staircase, and taken it broadwise, with the splinter bar toward the wall and the door toward the balustrades, and done it easy. There was plenty of width for that, and room to spare; which is perhaps the reason why Scrooge thought he saw a locomotive hearse going on before him in the gloom. Half a dozen gas lamps out of the street wouldn't have lighted the entry too well, so you may suppose that it was pretty dark with Scrooge's dip.[14]

Perhaps you could have lived a full life without hearing such a detailed account of Scrooge's staircase, but you may not suggest that Dickens is too careless with his words in painting this picture. Not a word is wasted—the mood, the humor, the voice, the space—cannot be better articulated in a lesser number of words.

Remember, we are not only the children of television, we are the children of journalism. We equate "short and to the point" with excellence in writing. But newspaper articles can only tell you so much. A writer wishing to evoke more must take you the longer way.

One of my favorite examples of the right way to dole out words comes from Alexander Solzhenitsyn in *One Day in the Life of Ivan Denisovich*. This novel provides a sparing account of the horrors of a Soviet prison camp, and it ends with the protagonist, Ivan, settling into his bunk to sleep. As he closes his eyes, he reminds himself of the length of his term: "Three thousand six hundred and fifty-three days. The three extra days were for leap years."[15] Solzhenitsyn shows his readers the desperation in just one of Ivan's days, and finishes by reminding us of just how many days Ivan faces—effectively delivering the knock-out punch in 14 subdued words.

Flows uninterruptedly

It is not enough, however, to use the right amount of words to contain a concept. The words you use must also flow. If the flow breaks down, well—Truman Capote warns us of the consequences: "A story can be wrecked by a faulty rhythm in a sentence."[16]

Is Capote overstating his case? Try picturing the goal of every good writer. I think it looks something like this: a tired reader lying in his pajamas, with one reading light on at two in the morning, muttering to himself, "I have to stop reading; I've got to get up early tomorrow" who just *keeps reading*. Properly understood, the goal of every good writer is to weave a spell—to draw his reader into a place that the reader won't want to leave.

Tolkien weaves his spells especially well, but my most memorable experience came from an author I don't particularly like. Late one night, I was lying in bed with my wife reading *The Open Boat* by Stephen Crane. To my mind, this is Crane's best work, and so I was soon drawn into a world with a few men trapped in a lifeboat in an uneasy sea. The spell was eventually broken, however, by my wife, who was watching me and laughing. In her own kind way, she pointed out to me that as I was reading the story, I was gently moving the book six inches further from my nose, and then back again—away, and back. Apparently I was so caught up in the story that my mind was in the lifeboat, moving back and forth with the swell of the sea!

And that. Is why. You can't write a. Sentence like this. At least, not if you want to weave a spell. It may seem odd to talk about rhythm apart from music, but good writing has good rhythm. Bad rhythm jars the reader and risks breaking the spell.

Unfailingly chooses the *mot juste*

At this point, the aspiring writer might well cry out in despair: I can't be too wordy nor too miserly with my words, and I must never allow a faulty rhythm to sneak into my prose—and now, on top of everything else, I'm expected to constantly choose the right word? Impossible!

To which I can only respond: you ain't kidding. I don't know how they do it either. But once you fully recognize how hard it is to do great writing, you can take a small measure of comfort in the fact that not-so-great writers like me are in the vast majority. Excellence is always especially demanding, which is why there are plenty of very good baseball players who never make the major leagues. You expect me to step into the pitch, looking for the fastball, but not to be fooled by the change-up? And to do all this trying to hit *behind* the runner?! Impossible!

And yet, guys like Henry Aaron could consistently do the impossible. Or, to get back to my second love, guys like John Steinbeck.

Two things are essential for obeying this trademark: a sizeable vocabulary, and a good grasp of connotation. You might say this requires a good "ear" for prose, just as writing rhythmically does. Consider this passage from Steinbeck's short story *The White Quail:*

> The blue air became purple in the garden. The fuchsia buds blazed like little candles. And then a gray shadow moved out of the brush. Mary's mouth dropped open. She sat paralyzed with fear. A gray cat crept like death out of the brush, crept toward the pool and the drinking birds. Mary stared in horror. Her hand rose up to her tight throat. Then she broke the paralysis. She screamed terribly. The quail flew away on muttering wings. The cat bounded back into the brush.[17]

Steinbeck knows what most of us forget: there's no such thing as a synonym. Words may have similar meanings, but they never have *identical* meanings. And the exact meaning of the word you choose matters.

High school English teachers usually put it this way: when writing a dialogue, you can always use the word "said." But there are so many other words to choose from: whispered, shouted, breathed, cried, spat, croaked, hissed—you get the picture. The best writers always choose the word that best fits what they're trying to describe.

Makes the reader sympathize with at least one character

No matter how carefully you sculpt your prose, however, you won't have anything unless you have a good story. As previously noted, this means that the author must use moral absolutes to drive the plot—but it also means that the author should create characters about whom the reader actually cares.

I used to say that readers needed to *identify* with at least one of the characters, but I've since realized that this is too much to ask. People are too different; there are so many personalities that you can't fit them all in a story (unless, perhaps, you're as careful as Dickens). A story will affect you the most if you identify with one of the protagonists, but it can affect you enough if you merely sympathize with one of them.

Still, this is easier said than done. Despite what most Hollywood "writers" think about creating characters, it isn't as easy as holding up a cardboard cut-out and trusting the audience to fill in the gaps. Real people are complicated— even more complicated than a brilliant analyst like Fyodor Dostoyevsky can describe. There are ambiguities on top of ambiguities in even the most straight-forward personalities, and a good writer needs to help his reader keep these in view.

Great writers are often great psychologists—that is, they really know what it's like inside the human psyche, and they can communicate it to us. Shakespeare provides the ultimate example, and not just with Hamlet. Think about how real Othello or Caliban or Falstaff or even minor characters like Cassius seem to us! We never struggle to sympathize with characters in a Shakespeare play—we're much more likely to struggle against sympathizing with the wrong ones.

Please notice, though, that what Shakespeare and Dostoyevsky achieve on a grand scale has been achieved by less ambitious writers. Kenneth Grahame creates at least four characters in *The Wind in the Willows* that are vastly appealing and real: Water Rat, Mole, Badger, and Mr. Toad. Isn't it odd that they seem "more human" than many of the human beings we think we know?

Rewards attentive re-reading

The time has come for C.S. Lewis to speak harshly. Perhaps you can bear it better than I, but it needs to be said regardless: "An unliterary man may be defined as one who reads books once only."[18] Ouch!

If you're like me, you're still trying to read all the great books for the *first* time, wondering how you find the time to read anything again. But Lewis is actually echoing something that has been known since at least the time of Francis Bacon: "Some books are to be tasted, others to be swallowed, and some few to be chewed and digested."[19]

The last category, of course, is the category of great books. Real readers will read great books again precisely because great books are worth reading again. What's more, the better we get at reading, the more rewarding the re-reading will be. What Lewis says of good fairy tales can be said of every great book: "I now enjoy [them] better than I did in childhood: being now able to put more in, of course I get more out."[20]

My own experience in this realm is woefully limited, but I can think of two examples: *Oedipus Rex* by Sophocles and *Murder in the Cathedral* by T.S. Eliot. While I was certainly aware of some of the irony underlying the words of Oedipus before he realizes his sins, each time I re-read the play I am astounded to find a deeper, more delighted irony infusing his words. Likewise, the more I read *Murder in the Cathedral,* the more I understand the significance of the fact that the actors who play the Four Tempters also play the Four Knights.

I expect that we could read works by Eliot or Herman Melville all our lives and still find things we've missed. But you cannot say the same thing for even a very good writer like P.G. Wodehouse.

Shows rather than tells

You may wonder why it has taken me so long to get to Lesson Number One in your creative writing class. This trademark identifies one of the most common mistakes that beginning storytellers make: spelling things out for their reader. Eager young storytellers believe they have good ideas, and they want to be sure that everyone recognizes how clever those ideas are. So they write with a heavy hand.

As creative writing teachers are quick to point out, this is a mistake. "No one can write decently," says E.B. White "who is distrustful of the reader's intelligence, or whose attitude is patronizing."[21] Good fiction writing doesn't *tell* a reader what to think or feel—it simply *shows* the details of a story and trusts the reader to come to the right conclusions.[22] If White does his job properly, for example, he knows that he can trust his readers to cheer for a spider in *Charlotte's Web,* even if most folks aren't naturally rooting for spiders.

This basic lesson seems especially lost on modern Christian writers. Far too many novels by Christian writers preach to the reader, rather than relying on the story to gently teach. We all want to write the Sermon on the Mount— forgetting that the pulpit is the place for sermons, and the novel is the place for parables. I suppose it's because Christian writers are so eager to help our readers see the truth of Christianity; but bad writing is bad writing even if it's done for a noble purpose. My first novel, *Ian,* makes me wince in certain places—the places where I abandon the story to poke and prod the reader—*You got that didn't you? You see what I'm saying here?* Readers would rather draw their own conclusions than have them thrust upon them.

This is especially true with regard to the characters in a story. The fastest way a writer can doom a character is to tell his reader the character is honest, loyal and brave. Right away the reader smells a rat. It's human nature: we don't trust people who tell us they're moral; we trust people who *show* us they are moral. F. Scott Fitzgerald summarizes this brilliantly in one three-word sentence: "Action is character."[23] Read that again. Now set this essay aside and think about it for ten minutes. "Action is character." How can something so deep and so terrible be contained in such a short and inoffensive sentence?

There is a sense in which I don't know anything about you until I see you make a hard choice in the moment of crisis. And there is a sense in which I know everything about you once I've seen that choice. You may dress nicely, keep yourself clean, and always have a kind word for others, but when the plot thickens, so to speak, is when you reveal yourself to others. This is true of characters in a book, and it is true of you and me.

Fitzgerald is saying something about writing that Jesus taught about life: "By their fruit you will recognize them. Do people pick grapes from thorn-bushes or figs from thistles? Likewise every good tree bears good fruit, but a bad tree bears bad fruit" (Matthew 7:16-17). Just as we know whether or not to cheer for Simon Legree based on his actions, we know whether or not a man is walking in the Spirit by his actions. John says in 1 John 1:6-7, "If we claim to have fellowship with [God] yet walk in the darkness, we lie and do not live by the truth. But if we walk in the light, as he is in the light, we have fellowship with one another, and the blood of Jesus, his Son, purifies us from all sin."

The author who wants to convince us that a character is moral needs to show us the moral behavior of that character, especially at the moment of crisis. This is part of the magic of story: the reader doesn't have to read about all the character's "normal" days where the character might be living behind a mask—the reader gets to cut straight to the key moments: the shipwreck, the death of a loved one, the temptation, the battle. The mask might have fooled us on a routine day, but it is stripped away at times like this.

And it is with immeasurable delight that we find the mask stripped away and a man behaving nobly. This is why we can love a character like Atticus Finch unreservedly: we weren't talked into loving him—we were convinced by his Christ-like actions at the worst time of his life. Remember how Atticus disciplined Scout? Or how he responded when Ewell spit on him? Or how he battled for the life of Tom Robinson? A man isn't wearing a mask at times like that.

Expresses the inexpressible

It is right to be brave and just and kind. Isn't this, at bottom, the message of *To Kill a Mockingbird*? Atticus Finch shows us the right way to behave.

But if this is the message of that story—281 pages in my edition—why does Harper Lee go to all the trouble? Why doesn't she simply publish the message: "It is right to be brave and just and kind"?

The answer, of course, is that her story expresses more than that. And if I could tell you everything her story expressed, she wouldn't have needed to write the story. Great works of fiction should express the inexpressible—that is, they should say the things that can't be plainly articulated in an essay or a dialog.

This explains, by the way, why novels may often be "art," but works of non-fiction rarely achieve that status. Art requires helping your audience "see" truth, and oftentimes seeing can only result from *experience*. Parents know the difference: a father can tell his child a truth over and over again, but sometimes the child won't see that truth until he has experienced it for himself. Non-fiction works like parental lectures; fiction works like the real world.

Moves you

Parental lectures help us understand truth on an intellectual level, but that doesn't always mean we've embraced that truth emotionally and spiritually. Sometimes it takes a deeper experience for us to do that. And sometimes that experience can be provided by art. A great book can move the *whole* reader—heart, soul and mind.

I may be able to write an essay that convinces you that it is good to be honest, but that intellectual conviction won't change your behavior. If I want you to behave more honestly, I must not only convince your intellect—I must make you hunger and thirst for integrity. How can I write an essay like that?

I'm not sure that anyone can. Instead, as William Kilpatrick points out, character education requires story.[24] To make my reader hunger and thirst for integrity, I must hold up an odd kind of mirror—the mirror of story. This mirror reflects both who the reader is and who the reader might be—if he is willing to bear the burden of Atticus Finch. And when they see the fruit of Atticus's life, they are more likely to be willing to face the trials.

This explains, by the way, why biography can occasionally approach the realm of art. Fictional stories can

move us, but so can historical stories. The proper telling of
the life of William Wilberforce can move the whole man,
too. Even more significantly, the proper *living* of a *life* can
move others. The "story" of your life, if you are walking in
the Spirit, can make others desire what you have—can, in
fact, be the most articulate apologetic for your faith. The
right life can be the highest art, as demonstrated by the life
of Christ. Just as no man can ever equal the creativity
inherent in God's creation, no man can ever match the
artistry of Christ's lived life. But to the degree that we
conform to Christ's image, we can approach that highest
realm of art.

This also explains, then, the "practical" function of
literature. Christians often make the mistake of adopting a
utilitarian view of things, acting as though we should only
participate in activities that are "useful" (as if climbing a
mountain is useful!). Utilitarian Christians are usually
suspicious of literature. If we *must* read, they huff, why don't
we just read the Bible? What possible purpose could reading a
novel serve?

Practically speaking, reading a novel can move us. It
can cause us to hunger and thirst for righteousness. Viewed
from this perspective, I can hardly imagine a more important
activity for the Christian teenager than reading *Cry, the
Beloved Country* by Alan Paton.

This also means that reading is a dangerous activity.
If great literature can move us in the *right* direction, it can
also move us in the *wrong* direction. A writer like John
Steinbeck can tell a brilliant story like *The Grapes of Wrath*
to move you to embrace socialism. Christians should
certainly read great books, but they should be discerning
about the great books they read. Not every great book has a
biblical theme.

Creates with a distinct voice

I have saved this trademark for last because in some ways it is the most distinguishing characteristic of great literature. Harold Bloom, one of the most influential literary critics of our day, writes, "When you read a canonical work [that is, a work that belongs in the Western canon of great books] for a first time you encounter a stranger, an uncanny startlement rather than a fulfillment of expectations."[25] He means that great books have great voices—they say things in ways we never would have thought to say them.

Bloom, in fact, treats this trademark as the only certain way to identify a great book. He links it, as I think it should be linked, to that slippery concept *genius*. What do we mean by genius? Certainly more than mere technical excellence. A book may be extremely well written and still not have a "soul." What gives a book the spark of life?

Obviously, the life must come from the author. Something about the storyteller's voice must be so compelling that it convinces us the story is important and true. And this is the sense (and the only sense) in which writers from Virgil to Shakespeare to Milton to Dickens to Tolstoy are alike. Their voices are very different, but they are all compelling. We recognize their voice each time they speak, and we are bound to listen.

Is it because what they have to say is new and exciting? Not at all. It would be more accurate to say that these authors discuss the old and timeless. What, then, makes them startling? According to Thomas Carlyle, it is their genius for expressing their beliefs: "The merit of originality is not novelty; it is sincerity. The believing man is the original man; whatsoever he believes, he believes it for himself, not for another."[26] It isn't that Shakespeare had countless new ideas; it's that he expressed himself so sincerely that we could hear and understand.

Consider Dickens. What makes his voice distinct? It's his sincerity about a few things: the uncertainty of growing up, the injustice of child labor, the dreariness of big cities—especially London, the vague haunting from a spiritual world, the charm of the foibles of real people. These are the concerns of Dickens, baldly expressed, and they recur constantly in his books. When Dickens "lets himself go" on these topics, his readers hear the passion in his voice and hold their breath. We listen closely because we hear a brilliant man speaking from his heart.

If this all seems a little nebulous to you, it should. Trying to define genius is a little like trying to defuse a bomb—if I knew exactly how it was done, I wouldn't be sweating. Even the geniuses can't tell you what makes them a genius. But at least we know what genius *doesn't* sound like: it doesn't sound like everybody else. What it says sounds fresh and intriguing, not because of the content but because of the voice.

The unwritten rule

So there it is—the checklist. Fulfill these twelve trademarks—check, check, check—and you've written a great book. But of course it's not so cut and dried as all that.

Skill will always be difficult to define. This essay represents my best effort, but it is by no means the last word. We know for certain that God wants Christians to be concerned with skill, because He charges us to dwell on the "excellent" in Philippians 4:8. Unfortunately, God never explicitly defines literary skill in His Word,[27] so we're left with the best efforts of fallible human beings.

What's more, you've probably already noticed that

some great books can break some of these trademarks and still be great books. Dante, for example, certainly does not maintain proportion and perspective in his tour through hell in *The Divine Comedy*. Tolstoy and Dostoyevsky often tell rather than show. But these failures to obey certain trademarks in no way take away from the brilliance of *The Divine Comedy* or *The Death of Ivan Ilych*. Great writers can break some of the trademarks and still write great books.

Which brings us to the unwritten rule, provided by T.S. Eliot: "It's not wise to violate the rules until you know how to observe them."[28] Although these trademarks are not the final word for judging literature, neither are they so subjective as to be irrelevant. Great writers always have these concepts in view when they write,[29] and they will generally stay true to them. Occasionally, however, a great story may require the author to violate some of these trademarks.[30] The great writers can get away with it.

Rather than focusing on these exceptions, this essay focuses on the shared characteristics of great books. In doing this, we are able to determine many of the trademarks of great literature—what makes a book "art." Christians should be glad to discover this standard, because we are commanded to focus on the excellent. But we should also beware: focusing on the excellent is not enough. The great books that Christians "swallow and digest" should also be true, noble, right, pure, lovely, admirable, and praiseworthy.

Does that sound like a call to hard work? No doubt. Fortunately, it is not a burden that we bear alone. The Christian can do all things through Christ, including thinking well about the best books ever written.

THE HUNT FOR HOPE

Blaise Pascal, the brilliant Christian author of *Pensees*, believed that studying the nature of man was one of the most important things a person could do. He was shocked to find that most people disagreed: "I thought I should at least find many companions in my study of man, since it is his true and proper study. I was wrong. Even fewer people study man than mathematics."[31]

More than 300 years later, Pascal's words still ring true—in fact, they hold a special condemnation for modern Christians because today many believers often ignore or misrepresent the nature of man.

What is man? According to Pascal, "Man is nothing but a subject full of natural error that cannot be eradicated except through grace."[32] Put simply: man is inherently sinful. All orthodox Christians would agree with this statement, but unfortunately not all of them would be able to tell you what it means.

Other worldviews also speak of the sinfulness of man: Mormons, Jehovah's Witnesses, Jews and even Muslims will label certain actions as "sinful." Some modern Christians recognize this and assume that the Christian view of the nature of man is the same as that of false religions, which implies that there's not much use thinking about the nature of man since other religions answer this question well and still draw bad conclusions.

Pascal saw things differently. He believed that the Bible's portrait of humanity was diametrically opposed to other views: "No religion except our own has taught that man is born sinful, no philosophical sect has said so, so none has told the truth."[33]   Obviously, if he is right, then the study of man matters very much.

And it should come as no surprise that Pascal was right. The only surprise is that the church has allowed so many Christians to forget this truth.

We need to be reminded of the biblical portrait of man's condition. Romans 3:23 assures us that "all have sinned and fall short of the glory of God"—that is, each of us is unrighteous. But not just because we behave badly! Scripture tells us that we are *innately* sinful; that by virtue of being a descendant of Adam we have the seed of rebellion in us from the moment we exist (Romans 5:12-17). No one can be good enough to please God because everyone begins with the stain of Adam's sin.

As Pascal explains, every other worldview denies this truth. *Every* other worldview claims that man is good enough—or at least neutral enough—to rescue himself by behaving well.

On the surface this might seem like a reckless generalization, especially when one remembers that some worldviews don't even promise heaven or immortality. What about the Humanist or the Marxist who denies the existence of the supernatural? Does it make sense to say that they claim man can "rescue" himself? Isn't salvation a purely religious concept?

Well, salvation might be a "religious" concept, but we should remember that all worldviews are religious—that is, all worldviews attempt to answer the most foundational questions, and all require faith (just think of how much faith the atheist must muster to believe that life arose from non-life by chance!). Once we recognize that all worldviews are religious, it makes sense that each worldview would provide an answer about how man can "rescue" himself.

The Marxist says that man may rescue himself by

initiating global communism. This won't make man immortal, of course, but it *will* be paradise. V.I. Lenin, the founder of the Soviet Union, actually claimed that global communism would require neither laws nor governors, because no one would ever behave in the wrong way![34]

Humanists make similar claims. B.F. Skinner imagined a perfect community he called Walden Two where one genius manipulated the environment so that everyone else behaved perfectly all the time.[35] Other more conventional worldviews feature more conventional paradises: Mormons promise exaltation (where human beings become gods), Muslims promise a sensual paradise, and most Buddhists and Hindus promise nirvana. A close scrutiny of worldviews reveals that all of them promise their adherents some form of earthly or spiritual paradise.

What's more, every worldly worldview promises that *man can save himself*. Does the Marxist expect any supernatural help in achieving global communism? Of course not. He expects that men conscious of the ways in which economic conditions determine circumstances can manipulate those conditions and usher in paradise. Likewise, the Humanist expects man to pull himself up by his own bootstraps.

Even worldviews that give lip service to "sin" ultimately assume that man is basically good or neutral. Sin, according to these views, is merely bad behavior and not something intrinsic to the human condition.

Consider the Muslim. He believes that when he dies Allah will weigh his deeds on a scale. If his good deeds outweigh his bad deeds, then he will enter paradise. Who performs the good and bad deeds? The human being. Who determines whether or not he is saved? The human being. Thus, we find an orthodox Muslim professor assuring us that "The idea of Original Sin or hereditary criminality has no room in the teachings of Islam…To put the matter in terms of modern thought, human nature is malleable; it is the socialization process …that is crucial."[36]

Mormons and Jehovah's Witnesses wind up saying much the same thing. Although both of these worldviews claim that it mattered that Christ died on the cross, neither would claim that Christ's blood alone atones for our sins. According to these pseudo-Christian cults, man must live a good enough life to be worthy of Christ's sacrifice. And if God expects man to be good enough, then man must have the potential for goodness within, as Mormon apostle M. Russell Ballard suggests: "The Church of Jesus Christ of Latter-day Saints discounts the notion of Original Sin and its ascribed negative impact on humanity."[37]

Even traditional Jews, who would acknowledge that the Old Testament is the Word of God, must ultimately deny the doctrine of Original Sin. Because Jews must rely on themselves to keep the Law to please God, they must assume that they have the basic capacity for goodness within themselves. Rabbi David J. Wolpe puts it this way: "Judaism is a faith that believes in the renewal and change of the human being…. We can remake ourselves because more than anything else, what we are is a product of our own choice and our own work."[38] According to Judaism, men are good enough to "remake" themselves so that they are acceptable to God.

The Christian view of the nature of man stands in sharp contrast to these hopeful perspectives. While the world promises that man can save himself, scripture makes it clear that *man can do nothing to save himself*. No matter how hard we work or how well we behave, our very natures create an infinite gulf between ourselves and God. The news, according to Christianity, is very bad: man has displeased his Creator and can do nothing to erase the debt.

But this horribly bad news, if we accept it, causes us to consider the possibility that the very best news—the gospel—is true. Once we face the fact that we can't save ourselves, we must begin to cast about for One Who can rescue us in spite of ourselves. And in all the worldviews in all the world, only One Person promises to rescue us even though we are completely unworthy.

The nature of man matters very much, because properly understood it points us to Jesus Christ. If we are guilty and cannot achieve innocence, then we need an Innocent Man to sacrifice Himself in our place. Mohammed didn't do that; neither did Buddha, Confucius, Joseph Smith or Mary Baker Eddy. Only one Man, God Incarnate, was pure and willing to take our punishment.

The nature of man is really one half of the most important news in the world: it is the bad news that causes us to hunt for hope outside of ourselves—a hope that rests in the nature of God. Until we really understand the nature of man, we are doomed to bounce from religion to religion seeking to save ourselves—a pursuit every bit as unrealistic as flapping our arms to fly to the moon. Once we understand the nature of man, we may also understand the nature of God and His abundant grace, as Pascal explains: "Knowing God without knowing our own wretchedness makes for pride. Knowing our own wretchedness without knowing God makes for despair. Knowing Jesus Christ strikes the balance because he shows us God and our own wretchedness."[39]

What you believe about the nature of man and the nature of God forms the foundation for your entire worldview. If Christians are going to effectively communicate all the hope and the joy contained in the gospel, they must begin by understanding their foundation, and the fact that it differs radically from other worldviews. The world may claim that some religions like Mormonism or Christian Science are very similar to the Christian view, but they are wrong. Christianity is distinct, and that distinctiveness makes all the difference in the world for otherwise hopeless sinners.

NEITHER BRAVE NOR NEW

When your grandfather is known as "Darwin's Bulldog" and your brother signs the second *Humanist Manifesto*, you would feel some pressure to accept the atheistic worldview. But Aldous Huxley, the grandson of T.H. Huxley and brother of Julian, couldn't bring himself to embrace a faith that denied the existence of the supernatural. Unfortunately, he also rejected Christianity, and so he became one of the modern pioneers of the New Age movement.

As you would expect, such a lineage and such a clash of faiths resulted in some interesting books, chief of which is Aldous's most famous: *Brave New World*. This futuristic novel speaks directly to foundational worldview issues: the nature of man, hope for salvation, power and government, and the clash of religions. But what it has to say about these things might surprise you.

In the first place, you may expect *Brave New World* to be somewhat sympathetic toward atheism, since Aldous's family was famous for championing atheistic causes. T.H. Huxley ardently defended Darwin and characterized evangelical Christianity as requiring "belief in a Supernaturalism as gross as that of any primitive people."[40] Julian served as the director-general of the United Nations Educational and Scientific Organization (UNESCO), and believed that Darwin's theory was so obvious that scientists no longer have "to bother about establishing the fact of evolution."[41]

Likewise, you might expect that *Brave New World* would serve as an apologetic for the New Age worldview. Aldous was one of the first Western men to recommend using drugs to heighten your spiritual awareness, and he proudly proclaimed that "It is because we don't know Who we are, because we are unaware that the Kingdom of Heaven is within us, that we behave in the generally silly, the often insane, the sometimes criminal ways that are so characteristically human. We are saved, we are liberated and enlightened, by perceiving the hitherto unperceived good that is already within us ...."[42]

In light of Aldous's beliefs and those of his family, *Brave New World* should have been a markedly anti-Christian book. It is not. In fact, it is an artful reminder that Christ is our only hope for salvation.

Futuristic novels have a knack for promoting the Christian worldview, regardless of the worldview of their author. Unless the future is described as a perfect paradise (and what does that really look like, anyway?), the new setting—as in *Brave New World*—will only serve to remind us that man cannot build a perfect world. Once the reader recognizes this, he must wrestle with the question: Why not?

The answer of course, comes from scripture: "For God has bound all men over to disobedience so that he may have mercy on them all" (Romans 11:32). Every man is sinful, so no man can usher in utopia. Only the mercy and grace of Jesus Christ can rescue us.

People can often push this truth aside in their daily lives, because they naively expect that things will improve as time passes. But novels like *Brave New World* and George Orwell's *1984* swamp these comfortable illusions by showing that the passage of time means nothing if the creation of paradise still depends on the efforts of men.

Consider just how bleak things look in Aldous's ironically titled *Brave New World*: although the "new world" has existed for 632 years, liberty is nowhere to be found. Marriage is forbidden, and procreation is left to science. Your genes determine your social class, so that perseverance, dedication and similar virtues are rendered meaningless. Those who question the rules or the rulers of utopia are threatened with exile to the Savage Reservation.

The stability of the dictatorship rests largely on genetic engineering—a suggestive idea for modern readers who know how close science is to cloning humans. This slap at the atheist's undiscriminating faith in science is blatant: Aldous rightly demonstrates that scientific advances made apart from an absolute ethical standard are more likely to be harmful than beneficial. (Ironically, his brother Julian ignored this slap and actually championed eugenics; in a 1962 lecture he recommended hastening the progress of man by encouraging artificial insemination using donors with "superior" characteristics.)

Clearly, Aldous's brave new world is not paradise. More than anything, it's a parable about the bankruptcy of atheism and the folly of unreservedly trusting scientific progress. H.G. Wells, a militant atheist, understood Aldous's message and was appalled; he wrote Aldous a letter accusing him of "treason to science and defeatist pessimism." Another atheist, Wyndham Lewis, described the novel as "an unforgivable offence to Progress."

Aldous's offence, of course, was his revelation that the emperor had no clothes—that atheism can't define morality and therefore can't make any judgments with regard to perfection or progress. But Aldous wants to make judgments, and he believes that his New Age faith allows him to do so. Thus, he introduces us to one of the oddest "heroes" in literature, John the Savage.

Designating John as a savage is another conscious jab at atheists; as the reader discovers, John is actually quite cultured and articulate. His "savagery" lies in the fact that he believes in the existence of more than the physical world—a "primitive" notion, from the atheist's perspective. Aldous is quick to point out, though, that this perceived weakness is really John's greatest strength, and the only hope for the brave new world. Although John ultimately turns to self-flagellation and suicide, it is clear that the things he values are the only things that can break the chains of this scientific, spic-and-span, rationalistic society. Atheism had its chance; the only hope lies in mysticism.

Of course, one can't find too much hope in a suicide. Aldous certainly tries to make John reminiscent of Christ, but his actions are too random and his end too hopeless to make the comparison valid. And yet, sadly, John's brand of mysticism is the best hope Aldous can offer his atheistic family, and the world.

As he was preparing to publish *Brave New World*, Aldous had no illusions about the state of affairs on earth: "It's a bad world; at the moment worse than usual. One has the impression of being in a lunatic asylum—at the mercy of drivelling imbeciles and dangerous madmen in a state of frenzy..."[43] In this regard, he was not deceived. But how hard to recognize the evils in this world without having the hope of seeing them overcome!

ON WRITING

The whale's belly smells so powerfully I feel I could reach out and touch the flabby odor. In the pitch black, the stench closes in on me, daring me to lift my arms. Two nights and two days I've sat here, feeling the pigment bleach out of my body, counting my toes and wondering when they'll be digested.

At least the sailors are safe. My God is a mighty and just God (who knows that now better than I!), and I felt the battered sea subsiding even as I felt the whale's mouth close over me. The sea-lovers will sail to port bedazzled by a confrontation with the real God, and perhaps that is enough. Perhaps my life was meant only to be a failure designed to open others' eyes—a call missed to call others to greatness.

Still I want more. After glimpsing the grand means God could call me to, I hunger to be used. At least, that's what I tell myself—but if it were true I would not have fled the Voice that commanded me, would not have endangered the sailors' lives, would not even now be bleaching and shriveling in a soggy tomb.

Perhaps, though, my entombment has taught me something; perhaps, free of this darkness, I would never again act outside God's will—I would rise to greatness, confident in His plan. If only I could break free, I might yet lead such a life. But here I sit (as I have for countless hours), unmoved and unmoving. I should scratch and claw the stomach lining, fighting for one more chance. But here I sit.

I wish it wasn't such a slow death. I wish I had heeded God's call …I should be fighting even now…scratching to get out…why don't I? Why do I just sit? Why…

I pray, I doze, and when I wake I'm better. Things are not as dark—wait! Things are *not* as dark; the whale's mouth is open close to the surface! I stand, I scramble toward the light, and then a powerful jarring force (like a ship running aground) hurls me toward the light.

I land, coughing and choking, in shallow water. Flailing to shore, I collapse in glorious sunshine. Rays of heat pound down on me, drawing whale poison from my puffy skin. In moments, the whale's belly seems a dream—three days and three nights from ages past. I am ready! I can achieve the vision, follow the Voice. Whatever God demands of me is His! I will follow to the ends of the earth, a man redeemed. Use me, Lord! Conform my will to yours and lay low our enemies! Redeemed! Alive! With the mightiest God to serve— I stand!

The journey to Nineveh is long. I take no notice. Dusty, weary days serve only to remind me of the call, and of the limitlessness of my God. Likewise, the jeering of the Ninevites only galvanizes my will. Repent! You may mock me and curse me, but I will continue to proclaim the truth. My God is the true God, and has seen fit to use me. Do your worst! I am unbowed. I drink from the Spring of Living Water.

The Ninevites hear. My words have meaning, even for them, because they come from the One who created all meaning. The Ninevites hear and repent and recognize (alas, too late for them) the inescapable righteousness of God. The message has been delivered; now all that remains is for God to display His might.

So I wait. And wait. And the Ninevites hold their breath, in sackcloth and ashes and fear of the Lord.

And the Lord forgives them. I hear the Voice remind me that He is also a merciful God, a God who loves. The righteous wrath is withheld. The might of God goes unseen, and I find myself again undirected, missing my call by the smallest of margins. Am I never to fulfill God's plan? Must I always be thwarted? I feel the whale's mouth close over me...

LET RIGHT BE DONE

Is it ever a sin *not* to watch a movie? Is it possible that a movie could be so excellent—in every sense of the word—that Christians are morally bound to flood the theaters?

The question never occurred to me until I watched David Mamet's film *The Winslow Boy*. But as I watched this film unfold, I experienced the same sensation that contemporaries of Charles Dickens must have felt when they read *A Christmas Carol*—the sense that I had just bumped up against a thing so brilliant that it would last long after I was gone.

The Winslow Boy is not merely excellent. It soars while loudly proclaiming the rightness of right and the immutability of truth—interweaving biblical themes while striking all the right notes in character development, dialogue, and pace. *The Winslow Boy* is the very movie that Christians have begged Hollywood to produce for decades.

Which raises another odd question in my mind: Is it possible that Mamet made this movie just to demonstrate that Christians are hypocrites?

Whenever Christians bemoan the evils of popular culture, they invariably say something like, "Why can't Hollywood make a clean family film that teaches good old-fashioned morality? Hollywood could make a ton of money, but they insist on cranking out R-rated garbage instead!" The implication is clear: give Christians what they want and they will line up around the block (a la *Star Wars*) to support your film.

So what happens to *The Winslow Boy*? Christians ignore it in their frenzied stampede to *The Wild, Wild West*. It

isn't even released in a fairly sizable city like Colorado
Springs. It appears in one theater in the entire Minneapolis/St.
Paul region. On the Saturday night my wife and I attended the
movie, it played to an enthusiastic audience of eight. In short,
Mamet demonstrated (whether he intended to or not) that the
evangelical community is full of windbags who give lip
service to impacting culture for Christ while in practice
following the world.

Is this assessment too harsh? Consider: *The Winslow
Boy* is rated "G." It demands to be taken seriously while
avoiding cursing, innuendoes, or glorification of sin. The basic
theme of the movie is clearly communicated to the reader in
language and on paper: Let right be done. The nature of
"right" is never in question: it is aligned with justice and truth,
and it cannot change. Interwoven with this central theme are at
least seven other significant themes that dovetail with the
Christian worldview:

(1) The Winslow family, when confronted by a crisis,
is forced to move from a life concerned with trivialities to a
life where hard choices must be made. This move from the
trivial to the purposeful forces them to "grow up,"
strengthening the bond between father and daughter, and
maturing the ne'er-do-well son.

(2) One difference between the genders is that men
generally understand the significance of justice and women
generally understand the significance of mercy. The tension
between husband and wife in this movie underlines this
distinction.

(3) Good men are willing to sacrifice everything
without hesitation for the right cause, but these same good
men will experience self-doubt when they see that their cause
demands sacrifice from those they love.

(4) We should never judge a book by its cover. The
apparently smooth and self-seeking lawyer is willing to make

tremendous personal sacrifices to support a just cause. His heroism is doubled by the fact that he humbly conceals his good works (Luke 6:1).

(5) The truth is knowable. Both the Winslow boy's father and his lawyer can ascertain with certainty that he is telling the truth.

(6) The truth is divisive. Some people believe the truth should shine at all costs, while others will gladly sacrifice truth (and truth-seekers) for the comfort of the status quo. Men committed to truth will necessarily face persecution.

(7) Never give up. The break-through occurs when everyone except the lawyer has accepted defeat. The lawyer is tempted by his peers to join the defeatists and graciously concede, but instead he strikes the blow that wins the day. When we put our hand to the plow, we can't look back (Luke 9:62).

Christians are terrific nit-pickers, but I defy the nit-picker who can find a nit in *The Winslow Boy*. It is just that well done.

Which means that modern American Christians face a challenge. Will we back our words and vote with our dollars for the movie we've been demanding for decades? Or will we continue to ignore it in favor of over-hyped McDonald's Happy Meal Sure Things?

Know that there are no excuses. It's not enough to argue that you never heard of *The Winslow Boy* and so you couldn't very well have watched it. Following Christ isn't just about avoiding the bad—it is about conscientiously seeking out, and doing, the good. Voting with your dollars implies not the cessation of voting but rather the active search for movies, books, and music that are worth your money. Being a good steward requires not just hoarding, but multiplying.

If you want to see good movies produced, you *must* support the good movies when they appear. To do otherwise is to send Hollywood the clear message that you like things the way they are right now.

Which brings us back to our original question: Is it ever a sin *not* to watch a movie?

Of course there are exceptions. Some Christians can't afford a movie, and some have committed to forego movies for a righteous cause. Still, there are quite a few Christians who watch movies all the time...

SCIENTISTS, DRACULA AND THE BIBLE

You're a grown-up now—you don't believe in Santa Claus *or* the Tooth Fairy. Most likely, you don't believe in Bigfoot. But what about the Loch Ness monster?

Put another way: if you believe the Easter Bunny is real, you're in trouble. And most of society would shun you if you kept talking about leprechauns, because no credible person has ever seen these things. We're less apt to condemn someone who believes in the Loch Ness monster, however, because a few grainy photos suggest that there's *something* in that lake.

In America today, seeing is believing. We believe in the existence of monsters like Jack Kevorkian because we've seen him with our own eyes. We don't believe in most other monsters because we haven't actually seen them. Americans today all hail from Missouri at heart: Show Me!

This is the attitude (actually, philosophy) that caused so much heartache for Dr. John Seward.

Dr. Seward is the brave, dispassionate hero of Bram Stoker's novel, *Dracula*. As a scientist, he spends much of the novel refusing to believe in the existence of vampires—although he is puzzled by strange circumstantial evidence like open crypts and victims with two puncture holes on their necks. Dr. Seward wants to get to the bottom of the mystery, but he can't discover a natural cause for the phenomena he has observed. And he is too cautious to allow for a cause that he's never seen or suspected.

The novel has a happy ending—the Count is killed, and his grip over the heroine is severed. But much of the tension and terror could have been avoided if Dr. Seward had

acknowledged Dracula's existence more quickly. In perhaps
the most telling passage in the novel, Dr. Seward is rebuked by
a friend for his obstinate disbelief:

> Ah, it is the fault of our science that it wants to
> explain all; and if it explain not, then it says
> there is nothing to explain.[44]

Dr. Seward's reasoning went something like this: Vampires are
not natural phenomena; they cannot be studied and quantified
by scientists; therefore they must not exist.

Is such a conclusion reasonable? Many Americans—
including many intellectuals—would argue that it is. You may
even be willing to agree: we know that vampires, werewolves,
trolls, and the Great Pumpkin don't exist because no one has
ever observed or studied them.

Technically, this philosophical position is known as
empiricism—we know things because we have experienced
them. All of us rely on empiricism sometimes. When we were
young, we learned not to touch the stove because we
experienced how awfully painful it was to touch it. Maybe
someone warned us about this, maybe not—but we didn't
actually feel that we *knew* it to be true until we tried it for
ourselves.

This way of knowing things carries over into our
adult lives. How do we really *know* we can't stand music
played by Nine Inch Nails? We experience their music. And
shortly—very shortly—after experiencing it, we know that
we despise it.

There is nothing wrong with a little empiricism.
Problems arise only when it becomes an exclusive
philosophical position. If we assume we can *only* know
through first-hand experience of physical phenomena, we
immediately rule out the possibility of the existence of non-

physical things. In other words, if we say that *only* seeing is believing (as our friend Dr. Seward did), then we not only rule out vampires but also souls, free will, demons, and even God.

Have you ever seen God? Do you know any surgeons that have cut open a patient and seen his soul? How, then, do you know these things exist?

The Christian responds, of course, by pointing to the Bible. We have it on good authority that God, souls, etc. exist. We place our faith in scripture, rather than placing our faith in the non-existence of the supernatural.

One of the central problems of our culture is that many people live their lives based on that second kind of faith. The 20th century's most sacred idol—science—is not equipped to answer questions about the supernatural, so most scientists assume that the supernatural does not exist.[45] These assumptions are handed down to the majority of educators, who do their best to pass them on to our children. "In our greatest universities," writes Phillip Johnson in his excellent book, *Reason in the Balance*, "the doctrine that nature is 'all there is'…is the virtually unquestioned assumption that underlies not only natural science but intellectual work of all kinds."[46]

Johnson argues that this philosophical position prevails because of the unquestioning acceptance of Darwinism: "A consequence of the 'death of God,' which is simply the realization that evolution is our real creator, is the realization that we can obtain knowledge only from science…"[47]

This deification of science is the cause of much concern for Christians. Many believers respond to it by attacking Darwinism and other evolutionary theories—an admirable occupation.[48] But if Johnson is right—and Dr. Seward is wrong not only in fiction but in reality—then the root problem is philosophical. Americans must realize that empiricism can only take them so far, and that we all rely on authorities to tell us about things we haven't experienced.

The question is not, "How can anyone believe in things they've never seen or experienced?" Everyone does that, from non-physicists believing in the existence of the atom to non-fishermen believing that trout are better quarry than bluegills.

The real question is, "Whom do you trust?" Can only scientists tell us anything meaningful about reality, or can teachers, pastors, children, and other friends help us to know things? More to the point, isn't it possible that the most reliable authority is not fallible men but an historically-accurate book that claims to be the Word of God?

Lives led by real people consistently defy the "science explains all" school of thinking. Even the most hardened philosophical empiricist, when he goes about the business of living day to day, relies on other authorities—even unscientific authorities—so that he can know things. Has any scientist ever observed or measured the laws of logic? Of course not—they are immaterial. And yet the hardened empiricist relies on logic every day.

The same could be said for free will, thought, and other immaterial realities. Scientists, and too many other Americans, have a tendency to rule out everything immaterial because they cannot see it. But to rule out all immaterial things is to rule out the existence of the very thoughts that cause you to conclude that immaterial things cannot exist. C.S. Lewis words the problem this way: "Unless I believe in God, I can't believe in thought: so I can never use thought to disbelieve in God."[49]

How do we know things to be true? Sometimes scientists tell us; sometimes we experience them ourselves. But sometimes we rely on other authorities. The scrupulous thinker does not cast off all other authorities—if we did that we would know next to nothing—but instead seeks to determine which authorities he can trust. It is one of the tragedies of our time that most Americans have enshrined one authority—the scientist—as infallible, while abandoning the only truly infallible source.

ADAM AT SEA

When a man warns you that he likes to deceive, you would do well to look for deception. Unfortunately, too many readers have never heard Herman Melville's warning, and so they tumble headfirst into his trap.

On more than one occasion, Melville voiced disdain for the superficial skimmer of pages—the reader who reads only for a plot, and ignores the author's subtleties and implications. What's more, Melville believed Truth to be a slippery and unpopular thing—all but guaranteeing that when he sought to convey Truth, he would say it indirectly, making it available only to the readers who are willing to dive deep rather than skim the surface.

Melville sounds this warning in a letter to Nathaniel Hawthorne: "But Truth is the silliest thing under the sun. Try to get a living by the Truth—and go to the Soup Societies. Heavens! Let any clergyman try to preach the Truth from its very stronghold, the pulpit, and they would ride him out of his church on his pulpit bannister."[50]

Melville's first point is clear: Truth is an unpopular thing, and can't be preached to the masses. But notice his underlying implication: Truth is not what the orthodox Church thinks it is, and those people who attend church to hear the Truth deceive themselves.

Take these two assumptions together, and you may rest assured that Melville's books will prove very puzzling for the orthodox Christian, especially if he is a careless reader.

Melville's masterpiece, *Moby Dick*, provides the best example of the confusion he engenders. Critics worry this book like a terrier, but only their conclusions get mangled. The biggest mistake is made by some Christian critics, who argue for the orthodox "moral" that the wages of Captain Ahab's sin is death. But by Melville's own admission, few truly understood what he was trying to say, and these Christian critics are deceived. He wrote to Hawthorne, "A sense of unspeakable security is in me this moment, on account of your having understood the book. I have written a wicked book, and feel spotless as the lamb."[51]

If the message of *Moby Dick* was straight-forward, Melville would not need to remark upon Hawthorne having "understood." And of course the obvious Christian reading of the book is disallowed by the statement that the book is wicked. Could it be that Melville is intentionally playing to his predominantly Christian audience while subtly mocking their belief that Ahab deserves punishment?

For the answer to that question—and most other questions about Melville—I would highly recommend reading *Melville's Quarrel with God* by Lawrance Thompson.[52] While much of the rest of this essay will sound like I independently plumbed the depths of Melville and discovered his secrets, I should confess that Melville hoodwinked me with both *Moby Dick* and *The Confidence Man*. The man who discovered and articulated the key to Melville is Lawrance Thompson.

Sadly, Thompson's work is largely ignored today, especially with regard to *Billy Budd, Sailor*. Although many modern critics may be willing to reject a traditional Christian interpretation of *Moby Dick*, they still view *Billy Budd* as a generally orthodox work. Thus, in a sense, *Billy Budd* is Melville's greatest success, because he deceived the most readers with that work.

It's easy to see why people would interpret *Billy Budd* in an orthodox light. In the first place, it was Melville's last work—written decades after *Moby Dick*—and as such presents the possibility that he had mellowed with age. More significantly, the title character bears many of the marks of the Christ-figure. Notice all the Christ-imagery in the scene where Billy is unjustly killed:

> At the same moment [as Billy's death] it
> chanced that the vapory fleece hanging low in
> the East was shot through with a soft glory as
> of the fleece of the Lamb of God seen in
> mystical vision, and simultaneously therewith,
> watched by the wedged mass of upturned faces,
> Billy ascended; and, ascending, took the full
> rose of the dawn.[53]

Pretty obvious, don't you think? And the very fact that it's obvious should make you suspicious. Melville liked to use obvious religious language to put an orthodox sheen on statements that were anything but. Remember, we should be expecting a two-fold deception from Melville: first, a superficial story to entertain the skimmer of pages; and second, a religious veneer to encourage the Christian to read his own meaning into a contradictory text. Thompson puts this bluntly:

> As I see it, the major problem which confronts
> the reader, as he comes to Melville for the first
> time, is the problem of recognizing, and
> learning to cope with, those different forms of
> artistic deception and hoodwinking which he
> developed and employed, because of his
> embarrassment over the heretical and
> blasphemous nature of his views.[54]

It's certainly *possible* that Melville abandoned his blasphemy late in life and wrote, as the critic enthralled by

conventional wisdom likes to say, a novel of "acceptance."
But did he? Thompson argues against this conclusion, and a
close reading of *Billy Budd* suggests that he is right—that, in
short, Melville's last book is his best effort at cryptically
mocking God.

If this is so, then the narrator of the story would be, not
the voice of Melville, but a dupe—a man who could tell a
story in a straight-forward way from a generally Christian
perspective. But his words must have an undercurrent of
meaning that diabolically inverts their surface orthodoxy.
Further, we should expect the symbolism in the story to subtly
support the inversion.

Thus, we find the narrator describing Billy Budd in
Christ-like terms at the point of his "crucifixion," but the rest
of the book undermines these comparisons and implies that
Billy is Adam.

Consider: Billy is often described in the terms of the
"noble savage"—a natural man completely untainted by
civilization. We meet him as he minds his own business on a
homeward-bound vessel called *The Rights of Man*; unfortunately,
he soon finds himself impressed into service on a warship, where
he will die an undeserved death. If we remember that the ship is
often used by writers as a metaphor for the entire earth cast adrift
in an ocean of stars, then perhaps it is not such a stretch to
view Captain Vere as symbolic of the Christian God—a God
who capriciously places Adam on His earth and in so doing
condemns him to death.

After Billy is "elected" for this task (Melville, whose
father was a Calvinist, certainly knew what that word
implied), he loudly bids goodbye to his old ship, *The Rights of
Man*. This seems significant, especially when we remember
that Thomas Paine wrote an essay with the same title—an
essay that assumed that man was basically good. Could Billy
have resisted this "election"? The narrator says "any demur

would have been as idle as the protest of a goldfinch popped into a cage."[55]

Our suspicion that Billy represents Adam grows when we hear that Billy's "entire family was practically invested in himself," and when he later tells a shipmate that he doesn't know anything about his father or his beginning.[56] This suspicion is confirmed when the narrator tells us that "Billy in many respects was little more than a sort of upright barbarian, much such perhaps as Adam presumably might have been 'ere the urbane Serpent wriggled himself into his company."[57]

But it's not long until the Serpent appears on the warship: Claggart's pride and his hatred of Billy make it clear that he represents Satan. The significant thing about this Satan, though, is that he is an officer of God (Captain Vere), and as such God is directly responsible for his actions:

> With no power to annul the elemental evil in
> him, though readily enough he could hide it;
> apprehending the good, but powerless to be it; a
> nature like Claggart's, surcharged with energy
> as such natures almost invariably are, what
> recourse is left to it but to recoil upon itself
> and, like the scorpion for which the Creator
> alone is responsible, act out to the end the part
> allotted it.[58]

Melville's message here is that we can't ultimately explain away the problem of evil by blaming Adam or blaming Satan—the blame rests with their Creator. This passage is perhaps the most overt snarl Melville allows himself in the book.

But undercurrents of blasphemy rumble throughout the story. When Captain Vere tells his crew that Billy must hang, the narrator comments, "Their captain's announcement was

listened to by the throng of standing sailors in a dumbness like
that of a seated congregation of believers in hell listening to
the clergyman's announcement of his Calvinistic text."[59] The
irony stands on its own, of course, but it becomes even more
ironic when we realize that, in Melville's mind, the crew is
literally in that position—hearing that Adam's sin will curse
all of them in the eyes of the arbitrary God, Captain Vere.

        The bulk of Melville's case against God is contained in
the unjust accusation of Billy and his undeserved death.
Satan—that is, Claggart—brings his charge against Adam, and
then God—Captain Vere—makes a very poor decision: he
brings the accused before his accuser, effectively pitting one
man's word against the other. Worse still, for Billy, is the fact
that an enlisted man's word could never be trusted when it
contradicted an officer. Thus, when Billy enters Captain Vere's
cabin, he enters a no-win situation. In effect, Melville is
accusing God of creating an innocent man and then setting a
mantrap for him, allowing the much more worldly-wise
serpent to accuse, tempt and condemn the overmatched Adam
to death.

        There's more. The "sin" for which Billy is condemned,
to the Christian reader's mind, is the sin of killing Claggart.
But it needs to be noted here that Melville did not consider
this to be Billy's basic flaw—rather, Melville explicitly states
that Billy's only sinful defect is his tendency to stammer and
clam up under pressure.[60] How ironic, then, that Billy is
condemned to death for the one flaw his Creator gave him—
the inability to verbalize a defense when wrongfully accused!
Melville's blasphemy is (to his mind) delicious: God made us
what we are and then sends us to hell for being that way.

        And Melville's still not done. Captain Vere knows as
soon as Billy kills Claggart that Billy will have to die for the
action: "Struck dead by an angel of God!" exclaims Vere. "Yet
the angel must hang!"[61] But instead of pronouncing this

sentence himself, Vere convenes a drumhead court and then bullies them into condemning Billy. When one of the members of the court points out that it's unfortunate that no one besides Vere witnessed the encounter between Billy and Claggart, Vere brushes away the comment by calling it a "'mystery of iniquity,' a matter for psychologic theologians to discuss."[62] Even more significantly, as Professor Harold Beaver points out, Vere's drumhead court was "threefold illegal"[63] according to military law at the time—a law of which Melville was well aware! Thus, the character representing God behaves both illegally and immorally (by Melville's reckoning) when he orchestrates Billy's death.

Vere gets what he deserves (in Melville's mind) when he later suffers a mortal blow in combat with a ship named— as if you couldn't guess by now—the *Atheist*. Melville is not content to mock God; he must see to it that He dies as well.

By now, it should be clear that the reader must reject the superficial interpretation of *Billy Budd* that makes Billy a Christ-figure and Melville a mellow old author who came to accept God's order. Judging from his final work, Melville went to the Judgment Seat with his heart set against God.

He left behind a lifetime's worth of great books— intelligent, dramatic, engaging and subtle. In this legacy, Melville left a warning as well: Christians should not automatically embrace anything that's stamped with a cross or an ichthus. We would do well to remember Christ's admonition to be "as shrewd as snakes and as innocent as doves" (Matthew 10:16).

MERCY VS. JUSTICE

Bible-believing Christians often are accused, especially in modern times, of lacking compassion. Non-Christians lament long and often that almost no Christian actually exemplifies the virtue of being merciful. "What the world needs," atheist philosopher Bertrand Russell complains, "is Christian love or compassion."[64]

Of course, the stock explanation for this absence of Christian compassion is that no one is perfect; even Christians sin. The world rarely sees Christian compassion because Christians—like all people—are rarely consistent in pursuing the good.

Such reasoning excuses the Christian—which is wrong. Technically, the Christian is without excuse; Romans 6:18 tells us that we "have been set free from sin and have become slaves to righteousness." It may be a truism to say that no one is perfect, but the redeemed Christian, by the power of the Holy Spirit, is called to perfection. Christians won't act perfectly on earth, but they are certainly supposed to behave better than the rest of the world.

So the problem remains. The world looks for Christian compassion. Christians rarely demonstrate it, even though God has set them free to do so. Why?

The answer, I believe, begins with the recognition that people tend to lean in two different directions: they either have a strong inclination toward justice *or* a strong inclination toward mercy. These leanings greatly influence the way in which we perceive the world.

Even after a person becomes a Christian, his personality still influences his spiritual growth. For example, a stubborn man will have an easier time mastering the virtue of perseverance than that of humility. Who we are still dictates, to some extent, how our new life in Christ takes shape. This does not mean, of course, that Christ does not radically change us when we accept Him as Savior; it just means that the changes that fit our old personalities generally "take" faster than changes that contradict our tendencies. An impatient, genial man has a more difficult time learning patience than kindness.

Likewise, our personalities tend either toward being merciful or being just. This generalization has been described in different ways in the past; the most popular description of this dichotomy is the distinction between deductive and intuitive people. Some people think logically; some think intuitively. This generalization matches our experience; most engineers we know tend to be logical and most artists tend to be intuitive.

For our purposes, consider the logical person the person more concerned with justice, and the intuitive person the person more concerned with mercy. The "just type" of Christian is the black-and-white thinker (if A=B and B=C, then A=C). In all matters of justice and practical ethics, the "just type" can discover the righteous position, and is not satisfied until he has discovered the truth with certainty. He is generally more willing to take a literal view of the Bible as the Word of God, because that is the only logical position for a Christian to maintain. Virtually every Christian labeled a "fundamentalist" falls into the "just type," since personalities concerned with justice understand that the conservative Christian position is the only truly just view. These people know right and wrong, and are quick to let others know that right and wrong exist. They do not apologize for being right, just as none of the righteous men in the Bible (St. Paul especially) ever apologized for being right.

The "merciful type" of Christian begins on the other end of the spectrum. Merciful people are very capable of "putting themselves in your shoes," and the shoes of anyone else they happen to meet. They are less concerned with right and wrong than with meeting other's needs—that is, showing people the love that Christ first demonstrated to us. Because they are more intuitive, the "merciful type" is more concerned with how others feel than whether they are right or wrong. As one might expect, this person tends toward a more liberal stance, because he believes the liberal position to be more merciful: more concerned with the down-trodden, more interested in serving than in protecting rights or distributing duties.

What category fits you? An example will help. Consider America's welfare system: do you like it or anything it accomplishes? If you're a "just type," the answer is "no." Even though America's welfare system helps a few people who actually need help, the "just type" is whole-heartedly disgusted with the system because it is not, at bottom, just. The coerced redistribution of wealth is anti-biblical; hence, the "just type" rejects the system in its entirety. The method is wrong, and the ends do not justify the means. The "merciful type" does not see the issue as quite so cut and dry. Instead, they focus on the fact that some truly needy people are helped by the welfare system. If this is true, they intuit, how can the welfare system be all wrong? While the system meets some people's needs, it must have some good in it.

Notice that both personality groups tend to make a mistake when responding to this question. The mistake of the "merciful type" is obvious: the ends, for the Christian, do not justify the means, and the means are definitely anti-biblical. This group, in an effort to be merciful, actually treats others (namely, those coerced to part with their hard-earned money) unmercifully.

The "just type" tends to make an equally grievous, though less obvious, mistake. They have a very difficult time responding with compassion to those people who rely on the welfare system, and especially those who abuse the system. Because the "just type" sees so clearly that such a system is wrong—and that abusing it is worse—they tend to snub everyone connected with welfare. In their just outrage, they have a difficult time responding in love to various people. But Christ's admonition is clear: "Love your enemies and pray for those who persecute you, that you may be sons of your Father in heaven" (Matthew 5:44-45). And ignoring this admonition is just as wrong as ignoring the admonition "Thou shalt not steal," which prohibits the coerced redistribution of wealth.

In other words, both types of people tend to demonstrate less compassion than Christ calls us to manifest. The mercy-type seem compassionate, but when their mercy is put into practice, it grows unmerciful. The just-type preach more compassionate policies because they have a better understanding of the moral universe, but their powerful convictions about right and wrong often shift their focus away from the real pain of a few individuals. Both types of Christians, in the long run, lack compassion.

Both types of Christians also tend to frustrate members of the other camp. Why does the just-type have so little patience with the merciful? Because the merciful cannot "see" what is so patently obvious to the just; ethics and public policy are very difficult concepts for the merciful. On the other hand, the mercy-type has a difficult time accepting the just-type because they see the just person as insensitive and often harsh toward people that disagree with them. The just person justifies his harshness because he knows he is right and others are wrong with regard to practical matters; the merciful person justifies his characteristically flawed reasoning by saying, "At least my heart's in the right place." But neither of these justifications seem proper to the opposite personality type—nor should they. Christians should not seek to justify their shortcomings; instead, they should attack them as remnants of the old life they have cast aside for the sake of Christ.

Remember Christ's admonition that we concern ourselves with the plank in our own eye. The just-type, because they are concerned with justice, see all the injustices perpetuated by the mercy-type—indeed, they have an easier time seeing the latter's failings than their own. Likewise, mercy-types have an easier time spotting the unmerciful attitudes of the just. But both the merciful and the just will become complete only when they, through the Spirit, vanquish their own sinful attitudes.

The story of the Good Samaritan (Luke 10:30-37) provides a model for reconciling these two personality types (which, not coincidentally, is also a model for becoming Christ-like). The just-types such as the Levite pass by the beaten man—perhaps because they are in a hurry to protest the IRS or the NEA—but the mercy-type shows compassion on him (earning Christ's praise). Notice, however, that this particular mercy-type also acts justly. He does not demand that Israel initiate a national health-care system to support the cost of caring for the beaten man; he does not require the innkeeper to look after the man at his own expense. Instead, he concerns himself with right and wrong in a practical sense, and pays for the man's health-care himself.

This, then, is the model for the Christian who seeks to be truly compassionate: if you tend to err towards the just-type, pray diligently and seek earnestly to learn the virtue of mercy—and vice versa. God is not solely concerned with justice, nor with mercy. Instead, He is both perfectly merciful and perfectly just. As Romans 11:22 says, "Consider therefore the kindness and sternness of God..." For some, it is easier to understand why God is kind—for others, why God is stern.

Which is easier for us is basically irrelevant; instead, we must concern ourselves with the difficult chore: learning what does not come naturally.

The world only sees true Christian compassion when Christians are both merciful and just at the same time. Justice separated from mercy tends to encourage cold legalism, and mercy without justice grows unmerciful. "As there are plants which will flourish only in mountain soil," says C.S. Lewis, "so it appears that Mercy will flower only when it grows in the crannies of the rock of Justice."[65]

Non-Christians everywhere hunger to see the Christian life lived—why else would the world howl so loudly at the absence of Christian compassion? The opportunity to witness to this hungry world lies primarily in the Christian's ability to balance mercy and justice. The merciful must act justly, and the just must strive to be merciful. In this way, each man and woman will grow more Christ-like: loving the truth, but also taking the time to love every individual we meet.

FISHING AND PREDESTINATION

God casts wide His net to bring every fish in the sea into His boat. How many of the fish can God catch in His net? The question is absurd. He can catch as many as He wills—He can catch them all. Do any of the fish want to be caught, and swim willingly to the net? This, too, is absurd.

But when the net is full and hoisted on the deck, all fish behave the same. They flop and they fight in an effort to wrest themselves from the deck of the boat to their "natural" habitat, the sea. They can't breathe in the light and air—they need the gloom. And so as the fish are cast on the deck, God allows many to flop their way back into the sea.

Some fish—the poor in spirit—give up flopping before they twist back into the sea. These fish are caught against their will, but finally they acquiesce to a greater will than theirs and submit to be caught. Are they better than the other fish? No, in some ways they are worse: they don't have the will to wrangle back into the sea. Do all those who wrangle back into the sea stay apart from God? Of course not. He casts the net again, and again He drags it full onto the deck. Some of the same fish who fought their way free the first time, gasp and die to the flesh this time on the deck. Some fight and flop into the sea again, only to be saved on the fortieth or four hundredth cast. But some, the rich in spirit, may constantly flop away from God's will and constantly cast themselves into the sea.

Could God keep those strong fish if He so chose? He may keep whomever He likes. But He will not force any fish to cease fighting and surrender its flesh to the Fisherman. If the fish will not submit, eventually God gives them over to the sea.

Does our choice, then, save us? Absurd! We all would choose the fishiness, gloom and cold of the sea. Who would choose to flop on deck in light and air, feeling the flesh die? Only the poor in spirit give up fighting and are rescued by the work of the Fisherman. Only those fish that hold still for a moment will be saved.

We neither leap into the boat like Arminians, nor find God pouncing on us and holding us till the flesh dies like the Calvinists. This is the mystery.

POEMS

ETERNAL BLUEPRINT

Foundation poured (untested) on the site of my dreams
Cracked and crumbled, threatening house with ruin.
I summoned a bricklayer;
He left, head bowed.
The carpenter came unbidden;
He hurried from the scene.
But he returned, with most unlikely help:
A blacksmith, bearded, burnt from his labors,
Rich with power.

"I know the house must fall," I muttered—
Not daring his iron eyes—
"But must all be lost?
Can't even my foundation be saved?"
The smith decreed:
"No loss, only gain."
The carpenter nudged me and allowed,
"Especially the house must remain.
Only cornerstone need be reworked—
What good is the beginning to no end?"
He pointed, I turned.

White-hot light smote the house:
Flames crawled over my dreams—
Found envy and leapt higher,
Burned fresh with lust and greed.
The full, hearty smith
Stepped into the inferno.
A bracing wind flew upon the scene—

Fanning the fire to a greater rage,
Carrying sounds from the furnace:
Hammer finding anvil, and the smith's whistled tune
(How sweet the sound)!

I fell
On my face and cried up.
Wind blew whiter—
Conflagration:fire:coals:embers
My eyes opened,
Found fine refined house phoenixed from dead ashes
On redefined foundation.

Strange; I hear hammer on anvil still.

SUBTLETIES

When over-eager winter winds arrive
To quake the aspens hung with autumn gold,
Some dainty leaves will leave those still alive,
And yellow fall to feed the loam and mold—
Low graves. But marked distinctly, crying hard
In color shared by fellow trifles: eyes
With jaundice, custard, mustard, bacon lard,
Newspapers withering under their own lies—
Sad company. Just shades apart, charade
That mocks the regal hue that cannot fade.
Has ever blacker chasm yawned as wide
As rift from gold to mute yellow? Can man
Or woman striding craven ridge yet span
The desperate depths and gain the lonely side?

PSALM 36:6

The mountain sheep lives
With cold cliffs, tundra,
Twisted trees crushed by thin air.
He stands dim against the grey mountain sky;
He scrabbles from uncut path to
Broken, shifting talus.
Sheep graze below
On thicker sun-warmed tufts of grass:
Soft, moist, tender.
He chops hard-bitten, stunted handfulls of clump-weed
Grows firm and lean,
Sinew-packed, with sharp lunges and steps.
Softness labors, gives birth to doubt—
Throws hooves from their aim.
Softness dies in pain—
Resurrected Steel;
Or
The mountain sheep falls
Down
To the warm sunflowered valley meadow.
Quick or slow
Death, or worse,
Dead to the unforgiving mountains—
Herded fat, soft, and satiated.

SPRING RAINS AND THE FIRES OF AUTUMN

Two "strangers here in reverent fear"
Brush fitfully together from
Apart and pause; flit back and come
To center in a pendulum.

The center holds, the dance unfolds
In rhythm and rhyme as strange as…no!
Yet stranger than the Dance below
The heavens: awed-ly free tempo.

A man undone embraces one
Becoming one as two desire;
As God again, with warbling choir
Weds water, air to earth and fire.

Now when flame dims and vacant whims
Blow burning passion's focus out,
Your spring within and dew without
Bids me "be still" and quenches drought.

And when my plodding path to God
Lies buried under logic's base
(My feet of clay), your breezes chase
My soul to stars your airs embrace.

The world still turns and our concerns
Are real. But mystic union grown
Has rendered worries overblown
And carves our love with wind on stone.

STORIES

THIN AIR, THIN ICE

Leadville, Colorado squats 10,220 feet above sea level—higher than the tallest mountain in 37 states. Only the hardiest trees survive at that altitude, and they bend and scar as they grow. The people are the same. Living is hard here—not just working or playing or loving—life itself is more difficult. The Bible talks about men being forged in fire; it is possible, too, to be forged by cold.

Though most small towns view newcomers with suspicion, Leadville is different. Here the bent and scarred townspeople bob and nod to everyone foolhardy enough to challenge the thin air. A visitor at this elevation is regarded with the same pleased composure with which the mountaintop guru welcomes the rare man seeking the meaning of life.

None of this mattered to Donald Podge as he drove his Model T past Buena Vista and Granite and followed the icy Arkansas River to Leadville. This was strictly business. Three months of winter (it'll be a cold one) was all he planned to see; three months and then he'd be back in Houston—hopefully a rich man.

* * *

The old man on the porch leaned over the railing, spat, and told Donald the Warfields would probably be happy to have a boarder. *Yeah, two roads on the left, third house on the right. Yeah, it certainly was cold, but it'll get colder 'fore it gets warmer.*

Donald drove past the Lake County Bank, noting its presence but reminding himself he wouldn't visit it for a month or so. There'd be plenty of time; no need to cause a stir.

Janey Warfield, a nine-year old copper-headed girl, heard the steps in the yard and answered the knock at the door. A big man with a grey vest and a dull tie stood on the stoop.

"Hello, there, young lady. Is your (ahem) Pa or Ma at home?"

"Yes, sir." She didn't budge.

"Well, uh, do you suppose I could have a word with them?"

"Yes, sir." She didn't budge.

Donald shifted his hat to his other hand. He was wondering vaguely if he should add "NOW!" to his list of requests, when Janey unglued her eyes from him, turned her head and yelled, "Mom!" She turned back and smiled.

Janey's mother bustled into the entryway, drying her large hands on a dishtowel. She wore a plain white blouse and a worn navy plaid skirt. She walked with her shoulders thrust back, defying her age. Sarah Warfield knew herself to be a fine judge of character, and she had decided the gentleman with the plain striped tie would be a responsible boarder before he had even summoned the courage to ask.

Mrs. Warfield was right: Donald led the life of the ideal boarder, keeping respectable hours, wearing respectable clothes, paying the rent on time, and often attending Leadville Community Church with the family. The only bothersome thing about Donald was that he never seemed to work. Mr. Warfield—Earl—was especially troubled by this. Sometimes Donald sat on the porch; sometimes he walked around town; sometimes he shuffled papers in his shiny black briefcase; but he never seemed to concern himself with work.

Cracker—the men around town called Earl 'Cracker'—felt sorry for the new boarder. He offered Donald the chance to help him mend the chicken coop, but a dizzy spell kept Donald in his room. When the Fosters across the way were building a stable, Cracker invited his boarder to participate two days in advance. But a bad back flared up at the wrong time, and Donald wound up just a spectator.

The missed opportunities to work never seemed to bother Donald, but Cracker knew they must tear him up inside. A man can only sit and walk and shuffle papers for so long, before the need to feel the sweat on your forehead and the knots in your shoulders calls you to work. Donald was awfully patient, but Cracker was sure even a patient man (even one who wore different ties that all looked the same) had to work sometime.

Janey finally asked Donald. He had taken to walking with her to school in the morning, and on an overcast day in early November, she looked at the ground and said, "Doesn't it bother you to have nothin' to do all day; I mean, don't you like to work?" She had tried to sound casual, but she spoke her part too fast.

Donald sighed. "It's hard to explain how I work," he said. "You see, I'm a businessman. And businessmen work most with their brains, which you can't see happening, but it does. Then, when the time is right, and you've considered all the factors and decreased your risk to the minimum, then you, the businessman, act. But even then you won't see me sweat. It's still mostly brain-work, and you don't have to sweat or strain your muscles to use your brain." He paused. "You don't have to worry. I'm responsible. I just use my brain like your Dad uses his hands."

Janey walked slowly, intent on the road beneath her feet. She took a long time to ask the next question: "So, what do you sell? Like the Fosters sell horses and Dad sells vegetables and hay and the stuff he makes, chairs and dressers and gates and stuff. What do you sell to make money to eat?"

"What I sell," Donald answered, "is the stuff other men...well, it's tough to describe. You're nine, Janey, and you've never studied economics and you think the whole world is Leadville. I can't explain it to you, but you've seen my money so you know it works. Just let me worry about how I earn it."

The next morning, Donald dressed in the same suit and tie he had worn when he arrived and, after walking with Janey to school, crossed over to Highland Street. From there he turned down Main Street heading south, and casually entered the Lake County Bank. He stepped to the teller window and faced a grey, balding man wearing bent spectacles.

"Good morning, sir," Donald said. "May I speak with your delinquent loans officer?"

"Who?" The older man squinted behind his spectacles.

"Your…your man in charge of repossessed land."

"Oh, that would be me. In fact, anyone with an important sounding label or name of president or officer of the bank would be me. Hell, it's just me and young Ed who run this place."

"Oh…uh, well…I'm interested in a piece of land north of here in the hills. Believe it used to belong to a fellow named Dougherty?"

"Lemme check …" the older man turned and moved carefully toward a file cabinet. "Should know this kinda thing off the top of my head, but I'm startin' to forget things, like what to bring Mom from the store an' …" He lifted a file from the second drawer. "I'm sorry, we awready sold that Dougherty property. I remember it now—damn pretty piece, too. Gotcher little stream runnin' through an' all…"

Donald stiffened. He rolled his head to one side to relax his neck. "Well, then, what about the place right next to Dougherty's—the Johnson place?"

The banker turned back to his files. "Seems to me like…" he muttered, "yep, the same fella who bought Dougherty's bought the Johnson piece, too."

Donald frowned mightily. He brought his black briefcase up on the counter with a bang. He fumbled with the lock, opened the case, and withdrew a dog-eared map of Leadville and surrounding areas. "This 'fella' happen to buy any other property in that same area as well? Did he *happen* to buy the old Sweetwater Ranch?"

"At's funny. Now that you mention it …"

"And Garrity's place, too?" Donald demanded, tracing the names pencilled on the map.

"Damned if he didn't …"

The briefcase closed with a slap, and Donald trounced out of the bank and into the autumn cold. His mouth was set firm and straight.

He walked quickly, head down, but without purpose. *Damn*, he thought. The word echoed in his head with every step. A cloud passed over the sun and he cursed it. He strode straight down Main Street, not glancing at the dusty barber shop or the signs announcing the arrival of the new Penney's catalog or the children playing stickball in the empty lot. He did not stop until he was a half mile outside town, and then only because the wind had begun to bite through his jacket. Stooping down, he grabbed a large stone and threw it at a grove of aspens. *Damn*. He turned around.

* * *

Donald opened the front door of the U.S. Post Office accompanied by the annoying jingled crash of the bells hung from the doorjamb. He faced a placid, gum-chewing Postmaster.

"I hear you've got the only phone in this whole town."

"Yep."

"Could I buy a little air time off you?"

"Air time?"

"That is," Donald faked a patient grin, "Can I pay you for the use of your phone? I've got to call Houston."

"You're livin' with Cracker? I don't see why not."

The old clerk moved to hand the phone to Donald through the service window, but Donald stopped him and asked, "Do you think I could take it in the back room? I'd like a little privacy."

The Postmaster looked hurt. "Well…sure. I just didn't think it mattered so …"

Donald opened the door marked 'Employees Only,' and took the phone and moved to the back room—a cubbyhole with a desk and a chair and not enough room for a wastebasket. He spoke to the operator and waited. Finally, he heard Rich's voice on the other end.

"Rich? You are absolutely not going to believe this…What? How'd you know already? Never mind. Can you believe it? I'm—wait a minute, does Dubois know?…No…NO…Rich, that's it. Here I'm supposed to haul down one of the cheapest, richest lodes of silver in the whole country and…He said I shouldn't bother to come back??…Oh…Oh…Well, I'm no miner, how…I know. But, dammit, Rich how am I supposed to know where there's silver in the ground if even these local beanfarmers don't know? I know…I know. I know I've got a lot of money in it, and I know I can't let Dubois down…All right, I'll do what I can. I'll call you soon…yeah. Thanks."

Donald clapped the receiver back on its cradle. The old clerk looked in the room and said, "That's an old phone, you know."

"Sorry," Donald said. And then, "Let me know how much I owe you." He stood up, kicked over the chair, picked it up, and wandered out.

After lunch, Donald spent the afternoon rocking on the Warfield's front porch. He forgot to pick Janey up at school.

But by dinner-time he was back to his old self—maybe even a little more talkative than usual.

"Earl," he said (he refused to call a grown man "Cracker"), "I thought Leadville was a mining town. So how come it seems like everyone out here's a farmer?"

Cracker looked at him. "Farmers and miners're different kinds of men." He chewed a roll. "Don't make sense to ask how come I'm a farmer and not a miner."

"But ..."

"Because I'd be a farmer whether I lived in Denver or here or in California when the Gold Rush was on. You see," he leaned forward in his chair, warming to the topic, "a farmer loves the land and's happy just scratchin' out a living and gettin' to work outdoors. But a miner, he don't like workin' atall, and would rather find the mother lode and go live in a fancy hotel for the rest of his life. You see, there's a…a," he knitted his tan, wrinkled brow, "a *fundamental* (oh, that's a good word) fundamental difference b'tween farmers and miners."

"Pass the corn, dear, while we can get a word in edgewise," Sarah said to Janey. The girl giggled.

"What I meant to say," Donald said, "was why aren't there any miners trying to get rich quick around this town. I thought Leadville's land was full of silver."

Cracker laughed a pleasant laugh—not musical, and without rhythm, but genuine. "Well, Mr. Podge, you kinda answered yer own question there. Everybody that thought there was silver in Leadville thought wrong, or at least found they weren't ever gon' get rich quick off it. Fact is, only a fool would still be tryin' to dig silver out'f round these parts."

Donald blinked. "Uh…uh, are you sure?"

"Sure? Why do you think twelve families up and moved outta town last year? An' fifteen families the year 'fore that? And that ain't countin' ol' Joe an' his dog an'

Timmy an' Jack. Fact is, Leadville's been shrinkin' ruther than growin' fer th' past six-seven years now. By God, why do you think lamb's down to four cents a pound here, and you can hardly give chickens away? Ever'body turned from minin' to farmin' or else moved away, that's why!" Cracker got so excited he moved forward and put his elbows on the table, drawing an unnoticed scowl from Sarah. "Mr. Podge," he spoke slowly for emphasis, "There ain't no silver 'round here."

Donald was in bed sick for two days. Janey worried about him, but her mom assured her he was fine—no fever, no chills, plenty of appetite. Still, Janey took it upon herself to nurse Mr. Podge back to health—bringing him food and telling him stories she made up in her own mind. She started him off with her favorite story, a story she had borrowed from her teacher and then made better by telling over and over to herself. This one was about the tortoise and the hare, just like the old one. Only this one had a lot of details about the race course—how it wound over the highest mountain and then down to a dry desert; how it moved to the Amazon river and finally finished in the North Pole. This one didn't have the tortoise winning, but it didn't matter because the tortoise made many, many friends along the way, and the rabbit (that is, the hare) won but he didn't see any of the country or pick up any of the local flavor.

When Janey finished that particular story, Mr. Podge was smiling.

"Did you like it?" she asked.

"I think so. I mean, yes. I just don't know if the ending's right."

"Miss Shaffer, that's my teacher, said it just won't do to mix up a perfec'ly good story and why can't I tell it right, but my friends all like it and say it's a good story all alone."

"Well, it's the teacher who gives the grades," Donald

said, patting Janey's hand. "Don't get on her bad side.

"I've got to think now, Janey. Thanks for the story."

Janey would give Mr. Podge an hour or two to think, but then she was back with another story. He smiled during her stories. He didn't when he was thinking.

Finally, on Thursday morning, Donald was well enough to walk Janey to school again. Sarah told him that Cracker was helping Pete Jerboz brand several head of cattle, and he was certainly welcome to help after seeing Janey to school—that is, if he was up to it. But Donald seemed to grow a little pale at the mention of it, so she dropped the idea and instead promised him a hot bowl of vegetable soup upon his return from his walk. Donald smiled, put on his heaviest coat, and set out with Janey. Sarah stood on the porch, waving and wondering how such a frail man could earn enough to live.

As soon as they began the familiar walk up Mule Road, Janey asked, "What'd you like to hear a story about today?"

Donald looked at her and smiled. "Don't you ever run out of stories?"

She shrugged. "No. Do you?"

"I haven't thought up a good story in years." They walked a few strides in silence.

"Well, what would you like to hear about then?"

"I'd like," Donald said, "to hear a story about something you wish would come true."

Janey told him the story. It wasn't a story about getting married, or owning a pony, or living in a mansion, like all adults think they dreamed of when they were children. It was a story about who Janey Warfield would be: a person who taught kids games their parents forgot to teach them, a person who took care of sick animals, a person who became mayor of all of Leadville and outlawed litterbugs, dentists, mean dogs, and money. And everybody liked what happened in Leadville so much they made their towns to be just like it.

"That's my story about what I wish'd I made happen," she said as they stepped onto the schoolyard. Mr. Podge was smiling, but it was a funny kind of smile with sadness in it. "Did you like it?"

"I liked it, Janey. Do good in school today."

Donald walked out of the schoolyard, then turned and studied the simple, red schoolhouse. He nodded his approval and moved on. The gently sloping streets of the town stretched out before him, rolling unhurried and uncrowded. Hooves clopping on dirt sounded far away. Every house stood proud, wearing its own different makeup but wearing the same word that blanketed the whole town: undaunted. *What a pathetic look*, thought Donald. *This place'll be a ghost town in fifteen years.*

* * *

When Donald picked up Janey that afternoon, she was apologetic. "Mr. Podge, my friend Bonnie was selfish at recess today an' it reminded me I was selfish this mornin' when I told you my story 'bout what I wished might happen. I told you all about what I wished for me and nothin' about just a good wish for everybody that might come true."

"Well, Janey, actually ..."

"Wait, wait, Mr. Podge. I got a good story now about a wish for everybody an' I been thinkin' it makin' it better all day an' I got to tell it while it's good." She paused. "Is that okay?"

"Yes."

"My story's 'bout a castle, but not just any ol' castle. This castle is made of ice. That's right, ice. Yeah, I know a castle of ice should melt as soon as the sun at noon hits it, but this castle's built right here in Leadville, see, where it's so cold ain't nothin'...I mean, nothin' could melt it durin' winter, and anyways the castle is so big that what does melt off in the daytime you could build back up in the night-time."

"How?"

"I don't know...yes, yeah I do—wait. People would love it so much they'd climb up on ladders at night-time to build it back up, just because it'd be worth it all to see it one more day. See, it'd be beautiful—not like a snow fort that some kid makes all kinda leanin' to one side and mushy, but perfect, with them towers and a big gate and maybe a statue out front and it'd be all glittery, like ice not snow, and so therefore...uh dazzling! You know, dazzling."

"And that would make people love it?"

Janey looked at him a little reproachfully. "Well heck yes, that would make people love it. Don't...doesn't everybody love beautiful things? See, that's what would make it such a great wish to come true, 'cause everybody, everybody in Leadville and everybody outside of Leadville who heard of it would come see it and love it and wisht they could live in it like a princess. Or a prince. See what I'm saying?" she asked, looking very earnest.

"Yes," Donald said. But he wasn't smiling at all. His brow was creased, like he couldn't quite picture it. Janey felt bad her new wish wasn't to Donald's liking, but she decided it wasn't so much her fault.

The next morning when they walked together, Janey tried to get Mr. Podge to tell her a story, to remind him that storytelling wasn't easy when your audience doesn't smile (or doesn't really react right at all). Mr. Podge started to tell her a story he had heard in school when he was young, about a lion that pretended it was blind or deaf or something so animals would get closer and he could eat them. But the story seemed to be just a whole bunch of facts and words strung together and by the time Mr. Podge asked did she know what the moral was? Janey had already lost interest.

Cracker spent the weekend helping Jerboz ("Hell, he's 80 if'n he ever saw a sunrise") brand cattle, and Sarah canned peas and beets most of Saturday and half of Sunday. Janey played a lot with Bonnie (who stopped being selfish), and Donald spent the days roaming the sloping streets of town (occasionally stopping at the Post Office to use the phone) and rocking on the porch. Every moment Donald wasn't in the Post Office, the Postmaster was telling customers, "That Donald Podge surely hates that phone for all the time he uses it. He'll clap that ol' receiver down as hard as a mousetrap on a mouse." The weekend passed gently, with only the wind blowing off the mountains and funneling down the old dirt roads to remind Leadville that winter was hurrying home.

Monday morning, Donald awoke in an irritable mood. He hadn't slept very well, and the conscious thoughts of his tossings and turnings were filled with Janey's description of that crazy ice castle. In fact, the first thing he thought when he heard Cracker's (damn) rooster crowing was, "I wonder if people really could undo the damage to the palace done by the sun every day?"

Of course, he ignored the thought and focused the rest of the day on solving his (real, not imaginary) dilemma. Even when he walked Janey to and from school he spoke very little, hoping she wouldn't notice how far away his thoughts were.

But when he awoke Tuesday morning, he was thinking of the ice castle—and the next morning, and the next. Finally, a week and a half after Janey had told her story of the castle, Donald mentioned it to her during their morning walk.

He had made up his mind to do it when they stepped
out the door, but he was shy getting around to it. He let Janey
talk about the Wooster's new barn cat and the stupid spelling
test Miss Shaffer made them take, and walked her to within
sight of the schoolhouse before he cleared his throat.

"Uh, Janey?"

"Yes?"

"I finally pictured the ice palace this morning.
Remember when you talked about that? Well, I...I didn't think
too much about it then, to be honest. But this morning, I just
woke up *knowing* what it looked like. It had...oh, never
mind." They stopped at the edge of the schoolyard.

"What?" Janey was excited. "What does your castle
look like?"

"Here. It's time for you to go to class."

"Wait. I wanna know if yours looks like mine. What
does your castle look like?"

It seemed important to her; besides, Donald really
wanted to tell her. He started, "Well, my castle had six turrets,
that is—towers. There was one on every corner and one ..."

"Right next to each side of the big front gate!" Janey
said eagerly.

Donald looked at her. "Yeah, it did. And then the walls
were high with a brick design all over them and the only
windows were actually in the turrets, right ..."

"At the top."

"Yeah. And the castle wasn't square. It was actually
like a square with three more squares attached, one on a side.
You know what I mean?"

"Yeah," Janey almost whispered. "Like a regular
clover only squared off all around."

"Yeah," Donald looked away at the mountains,
enormous and enormously close. "But none of that was the
biggest part of my castle. You know what the most important

part of my picture was?" He looked at her. "You know, don't you?"

"People," she breathed.

"That's right, people. People everywhere. More people than have ever been at the same place at the same time in Leadville. And all looking at the castle."

"I know." They stood together in silence, Janey looking at her feet, Donald at the mountains.

"Janey?"

"Yeah?"

"Do you really think people would like the ice palace that much? So much they'd come from other places to see it?"

Miss Shaffer looked out of the schoolhouse and called, "Janey, don't make me tell your mother you were late for school!"

"I'm coming, Miss Shaffer!" Janey yelled, and started to run toward the door. She stopped and turned halfway there. "They'll come," she said. And she smiled and ran to the classroom.

Donald didn't retrace his steps down Beacon Street. Instead, he paced, head down, toward Main. He passed Wil's Barber Shop without a nod. He stepped over the grey-muzzled retriever that always slept in front of Tom's Market. He didn't look up till he neared the Firehouse.

The Leadville Firehouse was tucked between City Hall and an old storefront. It always seemed that the storefront leaned on the Firehouse for support, which in turn sagged on City Hall's west wall. Not an inch of space separated the three structures; they crowded together like marsh marigolds on the banks of a high mountain stream—dingy marsh marigolds in the cold of late fall.

Two garage doors provided the only entrance to the Firehouse from Main Street. Donald hesitated, looked around, and then raised one of the doors.

"Fire?" an excited voice asked from the back of the garage.

"No, uh…no." Donald moved toward the back. "I actually just wanted to ask some questions."

A young face looked around the back of the yellow firetruck. "Yer, uh, staying with the Warfields, right?"

Donald moved to shake the man's hand. "Yes, I'm Donald Podge, and…"

"George Gunny."

"Good to meet you, George. Listen, I know you're doing important things and I'm not going to encroach upon your valuable time, but I've been wondering…how much pressure can you get out of the firehose on (ahem) this here truck?"

"More'n enough to make you think a dam broke, I, I like to say." George chuckled, then hesitated, then screwed up his courage and asked, "Whatta ya need water pressure for?"

"Um. I need it, say, let's say I need it out on that high piece of property on Colorado and Pine."

"The Ferrel property? Lessee…there's a good hydrant 'bout a block from 'ere, oh, probl'y 20 bucketsfull a minute. 'C-course, I could be wrong either way. How come?"

"It's a secret for now, okay, George? But when it's not, you'll be the first to know. And, oh, I've been thinking— who's the best carpenter in town? Say, if I wanted someone to build a (that is, my) house?"

"I'd say it's Jerry Murphy. But others'll tell you otherwise. Cracker, of course (oh yeah, you live with him) Cracker'll tell you it's him, and might be right. C-Course, I'm partial to Murphy 'cause he built my sister's place, and there's never been a thing wrong with it. Then, of course…"

"George, I know the kind of responsibility you face every day, so I won't keep you any longer. Thanks so much for your time." Donald had his hand on the garage door by the time George managed a "No problem!"

* * *

Cracker washed his face in the clean porcelain sink, and then turned toward Sarah. She lay propped up on a pillow in bed. "What does Mr. Podge do for a livin' again?"

Sarah closed her Bible. "He says he works for an 'entrepreneurial' firm in Houston."

"What's that mean?"

"Near as I can tell, they give him money and tell him to use it to get more."

"You know what he's askin' me tonight?"

Sarah looked at him.

"He's askin' me how many people there are in town 'thout jobs. I said, 'Countin' you or not countin' you?' and he laughed, but he kep' after me. An' I'm not the only one he's been askin' crazy questions. Started with ol' Gunny at the Firehouse a week ago, askin' how much water his hose can carry; and then he's askin' Jerry how much to build a house and askin' the Bank who owns the Ferrel property. What's he gettin' at?"

Sarah smiled. "Well, if what Janey tells me's true, you wouldn't believe it."

Cracker crawled into bed and kissed his wife on the cheek. "Honey, I don't believe half the things you tell me," he said, and he blew out the lamp.

* * *

Snow fell in a soft, silent fury all night, and by morning Janey and Mr. Podge had to wear galoshes to go to school. All of Leadville was unnaturally still, missing the sound of hooves and voices. When Janey spoke, it was in a hushed voice.

"I figured out what would make a great insides to the Ice Palace."

"I thought it would just have a lot of booths filled with souvenirs and maybe a man that'll take pictures for a fee."

Janey wrinkled her nose, the way she did when she found a carrot in her stew. "Ick, no, Mr. Podge. This is a huge palace! 'Member, it's gonna be dazzling outside why shouldn't it be inside too? And see, so I was thinkin', what would be the greatest for my wish on the inside? And I thought, it's a castle made of ice, how 'bout a ice rink inside? I mean, a skating rink where people could come and skate anytime, and maybe have fancy skaters do a show sometimes, with costumes and feathers and everything?"

No smile from Mr. Podge, just a furrowed brow—but Janey knew now that meant he was looking real hard in his mind to see her story.

"And that's not all. See, that's just one room—the center part of the square clover. So people come in and see this big ol' skatin' rink, but then they got a choice of three more rooms—and every other room is great, too."

"Don't tell me. A circus in one, with elephants and tigers and people eating flaming swords."

Janey laughed. "No I wasn't thinkin' of that. But it's a good idea. I was thinkin' of one room bein' a big ballroom with a fancy wood floor and a stage for the band with the violins an' all. An' then another room that's a fancy dinin' room with white tablecloths an' flower cen'rpieces an' waiters in suits. An, then I was thinkin' maybe the third room could be a place that shows those new movin' pictures—like a theater, you know?" She paused. "What do you think?"

"I think Miss Shaffer's standing there to see that you

get to class on time. Get along." He patted her clumsily on the shoulder.

* * *

City Hall was as cold as the streets outside. Like most City Halls it was built too expansively—high ceilings and wide corridors without carpeting. Donald had walked directly to City Hall from school, and now wandered rather aimlessly throughout the building, looking for the Mayor's office. He finally found it after climbing a wide flight of stairs and walking nearly to the back of the building. Faded letters on the door's window proclaimed: Bob Simons, Mayor, City of Leadville. Donald rapped on the glass and walked in.

Twenty minutes later, he closed the door and marched through the corridors to the sunshine outside. Breathing deeply, he tapped his foot three times on the top of the steps and then moved down into the street.

* * *

"Marcy called me a big fat liar today," Janey sobbed, holding on to her mother's skirt.

Sarah played with Janey's hair. "Well, now, I wouldn't say you were big or fat, dear." She smiled down at her.

The young girl sniffled. "That isn't…Mom, that's not the…point." More tears. "She said…I was a liar…'cause I said…sniff…that we were gonna build a…super-fancy Ice Palace this winter…She said I was just sayin' that…to make me sound…import'nt and make me a big shot."

"Oh, Janey." Sarah looked down at her again. "Janey, some people don't believe your dreams till your dreams come true." She knelt down and searched her daughter's face with her eyes. "You can't…you can't tell people what you want to happen sometimes because it might be too…fantastic till they see it with their own two eyes."

"But I'm not a liar!" Janey looked quickly into her mother's eyes. "Mr. Podge said it would happen and I believe him!"

"I know, dear, I know. But people don't like believing in different, far-away things."

"But that doesn't make me a liar!"

Sarah smiled gently. "No, dear. All it really does is make Marcy mean."

* * *

The Warfields ate dinner without Donald the next four evenings in a row ("What the hell d'you expect?" Cracker told Sarah, "You're cookin's enough to scare off anybody!"). The Texas businessman was spending a lot of time with Jerry Murphy, even into the dinner hour. When Donald finally reappeared at the Warfield's dinner table, Cracker was ready for him.

"Well, well, well," he winked at Sarah. "I hear we're havin' a town council meetin' tomorrow night. Crazy. We weren't s'posed to have another meetin' till December to plan the Christmas nattivity scene. Now I wonder what this here meetin' could be all about?" He looked at Donald, who was looking at his potato. "Gee whiz, Ma, you don't spose Donald'd have any idea?"

Cracker grinned as Donald fidgeted. "I don't suppose you already know, Earl," Donald murmured.

"How's that?"

Donald rolled his shoulders back and straightened up. "We're having a council meeting," he said, "because I'm trying to sell Leadville on the craziest business idea ever dreamed up. You already know about it: an Ice Palace.

Now I've got some questions to ask, since we've got it out
in the open. Will the weather stay cold enough? How many
days could it last? How much manpower do I need to build
it? And most important, will people pay to go inside it?"

Janey let out a small gasp. "You're going to charge
people to go inside?" Her eyes were wide.

"Of course," Donald said. "Janey, it's going to cost
probably $1,200 to build and maintain. I've got to get that
money back somehow."

Janey looked at her plate. Cracker drank the last of
his coffee and then put his callused, clumsy hands together
in front of him. He looked at Donald and said, "It'll stay
cold enough. Figure you got from now through 'bout mid-
April. The more time yer willin' to spend gettin' it ready,
the fewer men it'll take. If you give me three weeks and
just two men, I could frame an awful big place. Really ain't
no problem in any o' that. But will people come? Will they
come? They'll come first off, like anybody does to any
freak sideshow—but will they come back? Hell if I know.
Seems like some of the crap games 'round here 'd be a
better gamble."

"That's pretty much the same answer I get
everywhere."

Cracker spread his hands, palms up. "Well, Donald, I
ain't no gypsy fortune-teller. An' there ain't too
much...*precedent* for an ice palace in these parts."

"Will you go to the meeting with me tomorrow night?"

"Son, I wouldn't miss it for all the tea in China."

When the rooster crowed the next morning, Donald
opened his window and threw a book at it. His night's sleep
had been shallow, moored hopelessly close to consciousness.
He woke up knowing that the palace was crazy, like a cheap
circus stunt. Even the beanfarmers knew that.

When Cracker banged on his door, Donald reached for

another book. But he checked himself and growled, "Come in."

Cracker had waited as long as he could to wake his boarder. "I know what ya need today, Donald. Ya need a good hard day of work to take your mind off t'night. I'm goin' to dig some stumps outtova field, and you can jes' throw on some clothes and run out there an' meet me. Sarah'll pack your lunch. Okay?"

"Yeah, Earl. I mean, that would be okay if ..."

"See ya there." He was gone, striding quickly down the hall.

Nnnnnn. Donald ground his teeth. *What I needed was more grief today.* He dragged himself out of bed and put on his old black pants. Then he sat down at his desk and opened the bottom drawer. The plans were still there, and the Palace looked just like it did in his mind when he first saw it: a squared-off clover with high turrets. But where were the people?

Donald finished dressing and walked into the kitchen. "Good morning," he said to Sarah, feeling conscious of his morning stubble.

"What can I get you for breakfast this morning?"

"Just coffee, please. Look, Sarah, I told Earl I'd be out to help him...work the field this morning but I'd forgotten I still need to go to the library and the bank before the meeting. Can you somehow get the word to him?"

"I'll tell him when I bring him lunch." She paused. "Neither the bank nor the library are open till nine, though, if..."

"Oh, yeah. Yeah, it's just I've got to work on my presentation till then. I'll be in my room." He picked up his coffee cup and shuffled out.

Once in his room, he lay back on his bed and stared till 9:00. Later, he spent half an hour at the library and five minutes at the bank—and the rest of his time at the Firehouse.

* * *

The town council meeting went well and was humiliating at the same time. Every townsperson in attendance (which was basically every adult within a 20-mile radius) was very cordial toward Donald—but the businessman had the uncomfortable feeling that it was the same kind of respect they showed unbroken horses. *Good idea, good idea...now just hold still while we slip this bridle on*...Donald knew he would have reacted the same way to such an outlandish idea.

He comforted himself with the knowledge that his presentation was polished. The Ferrel property actually belonged to the bank, which was willing to rent it for $25 a month. The plans for the ice castle were both professional and feasible, thanks to Jerry Murphy. Water wouldn't be a problem. And heaven knows it's cold enough.

Cracker rose to the occasion. He talked and talked (hell, he'd talk about anything) about how this "crazy idea" just might put Leadville on the map again. And hey, "It ain't gonna cost us nothin' if it don't!" By the end of the evening, he'd rounded up ten men ("damn good workers, too") willing to do anything for Donald's rate of $3 a day.

Yes, the actual presentation had gone well, and Cracker played his fiery part, but none of that clinched the vote. George Gunny, the lanky, black-haired Fire Marshall, coaxed the bridle off the horse. Just before the vote, Donald stepped to the podium and added, "I almost forgot. My operation will be too large for myself to manage, so I've created a secretary-treasurer position. And the man I've selected to fill that position is—George Gunny!"

The crowd had actually chuckled. "Gunny?" someone cried. "He wouldn't know ice if he found it in his drawers!"

Gunny stepped forward. "I seen an ice castle before. In Montreeawl. When I visited my aunt. You know I been there!"

"Gunny?" the crowd hooted. They razzed him and he defended himself for five full minutes before order was restored. He wasn't Lancelot, but Leadville loved him. Donald had picked the Vice President that assured him the Presidency.

Still, despite the unanimous vote, Donald felt more like he'd won a popularity contest than the confidence of the community. He'd delivered a presentation that would have knocked them dead at the board meeting, but no one in Leadville seemed particularly impressed with polish or break-even analyses. They nodded and smiled when he explained that his variable costs were so low he needed only to recoup a shade more than his fixed costs, but they weren't sold. And they kept asking the same questions: Are people going to pay to go in? How many people you figure'll come? Are people gonna go during the week, when they should be working?

Not that it mattered, he told himself. All he needed from the town council was vague approval, and perhaps enough interest to generate excitement with the hicks. That, and a trainload of luck. *Dammit. Staying awake all night wasn't going to help matters.*

* * *

George sat in the chair at Wil's Barber Shop. Wil stood behind him, aimlessly clicking his scissors together. Then he looked at Mr. Felkins sitting against the wall and winked.

"George," Wil said, "what the hell do you know about building an ice castle?"

"Yeah," Felkins sat up. "How do you s'pose you're gonna do that anyway?"

"Well…"

"I mean, George, you don't know the first thing about architecture. And what if the weather warms up? How are you going to keep the roof from caving in? Say, George, speak up."

George Gunny hunched his shoulders. "We'll do it," he said seriously. "I seen an ice palace in Montreeawl, and Donald Podge figured all the details. We'll do it."

* * *

The only newspaper in town, the *Leadville Telegraph,* loved the ice palace for two reasons. Not only was the palace the most exciting thing to hit town since the Golden Donkey Saloon, but the Palace also needed advertising, and advertising meant flyers and pamphlets printed by the only print shop in town: the *Telegraph.* Donald was in the shop at least twice a day, preparing flyers for Denver Rotary clubs and Colorado Springs sewing circles and every other group in the state. To the editor's mind, money poured from Donald's pockets into his shop.

The *Telegraph's* editor was just as dismayed as Donald, then, by his paper's recent weather reports. The sun had burned off all cloud cover, and was forcing warmer temperatures each day. As the week wore on, the noontime reached 50 degrees. The heat made Donald sweat.

But he wasn't sweating from overwork, as Cracker was quick to point out. Oh, sure, he went to the printer now and again, but mostly he just sat on the porch, rocking and looking nervous. Sarah said he was planning, which was okay, except planning without carrying out the plan can make you crazy. Cracker knew a good hour's planning could really only be cured by a good day's work.

And here was Donald, still finding time to walk Janey to school. In fact, he refused to miss a day anymore.

"I had a great idea for our Castle last night," Janey said as she smiled up at Mr. Podge.

"I hope it's not like that blimp idea you had yesterday."

"It's not…That was kinda stupid, wasn't it? No this's a good one. See, you have a big bobsled run that goes from the side of the castle all the way down, a mile, to the bottom an' then you have a horse 'n buggy to pull the folks back up. An' I can see you don't think it'd work, but it would…"

"It would, huh?"

"Yeah, because you picked the highest piece of land in all of Leadville…"

"So everyone could see the Palace."

"Yeah, but it also means it's all downhill, an' so you could dig out a track no problem an' then use my dad's team to pull people back up, and you could even pay boys my age 5 cents an hour to pull the bobsled back to the top. See?"

"And where would I find boys willing to work so hard for only a nickel an hour?"

"I awready found 'em. I asked some boys in my class and they said they'd dig a tunnel to China for 5 cents per. An' I asked only nice boys, hard workin' ones …"

"Ones without cooties?"

Janey rolled her eyes. "I know boys don't have cooties." She walked a couple paces and muttered, "'Cept maybe Scott Myers."

* * *

Cracker was a sport. If it hurt him when he discovered

his boarder chose Murphy to draw up the plans for the Palace, he didn't show it. He blinked once, and then he began slowly writing a list of supplies. When Donald approached him about overseeing the construction, Cracker had already ordered the lumber. He didn't understand Donald's bewildered and awkward rejoicing at the news; he was a man who did what he could.

Neither did he understand Donald's dismay over the warm weather. "Hell," he told young Jake (the hardest worker on his crew, and the man with whom he was most terse), "workin' in yer shirtsleeves beats workin' in a parka. And we gotta get the guts built afore we kin ice 'er up anyway."

And so Cracker and his men began work on the skeleton of the Leadville Ice Palace. No foundation was poured; the ice would have to provide the base. Instead, the rooms were framed and then the men began erecting vertical beams to support the towers. Jake and his apprentice could set a beam faster than anyone except Cracker. And no one said a word about it.

Donald often stopped by, and he seemed cheered by the progress. He asked a lot of questions, but never lifted a two-by-four or drove a nail. Some of the crew privately deemed him a slacker, but their foreman was quick to defend him: "Oh, he works alright. Just differ'nt than us. Uses his head, not his back. But he works." Cracker never was specific about Donald's work—he just told the men they wouldn't understand. Who could?

In a week, the framework was close enough to completion that Cracker felt he could send some men to cut ice from the ponds. When Donald heard, he fretted.

"Earl, I know the temperature's dropping and all, but it still was 42 yesterday. How can you be sure there will be ice in the ponds?"

"Hell, I didn't send the boys to...Hell, nor even

Arizona. I sent 'em to the foothills, Donald, where the nights are colder and there's plenty of ice. Don't you worry, I been thinkin'." He spat.

That was the only time Cracker lost his patience with the man from Houston. He could take a lot, but he couldn't take men fussing like hens. Donald understood.

* * *

"I got another idea."

"You're kidding." Donald tried to look astonished.

Janey giggled. "No, I'm not. (Stop lookin' goofy)—I figured you could have comp'titions t' get more people to the Castle. Like a ice-buildin', uh…sculpting comp'tition where people build statues and dragons and hounddogs outta snow to get judged to see who's best."

Donald looked hard at the horizon.

* * *

The framework for the Castle was immense. It covered almost three acres, and the vertical beams for the turrets reached 90 feet in the air. To Donald's impatient eye, it looked as though it would take all winter to haul enough ice to cover the guts, but Cracker and his men never gave it a thought. *Ya lay the blocks on top of one another, and afore ya know it ya got a wall.*

Teams of horses hauled the ice blocks from Stewart's Pond and White Lake. The blocks were generally cut in two sizes: a standard 2 foot by 3 foot for basic work, and a more delicate 10" by 8" for corners and joints. The ice melted a bit en route, but that only made it "stickier." Besides, Gunny was out every night with his fire hose, finishing Cracker's rough work. Donald was concerned that George might find the job a bit lonesome or tedious, but he needn't have worried. George knew that only people without important jobs got bored, and besides, children flocked to the solitary fireman each evening, fascinated by his part in the dream. Occasionally, too, an adult would stop by, asking "Where's the fire?" in the early weeks, and later in the winter commending him on a job well done. Gunny answered every comment or question with a grin and a foot-shuffle.

* * *

Item, *Leadville Telegraph*, opinion page: "This writer cannot help but wonder: if one of the ice walls should fall and kill a man, would a coroner's jury bring a verdict of death from hard drink?"

* * *

"Okay, I see that grin," Donald said. "What's your latest brainstorm?"

"It's not a brainstorm, really. I was just thinkin' 'bout how the Castle is…I mean, I was *looking* at it actually—you know, the picture we see. Have you looked close at it? Real close? The inside's got stuff frozen in the walls so that you kin see it on the inside but not on the out, like so you're lookin' through a window at things in the wall. You know?"

"Yes…I see what you're saying. But what exactly's in the wall?"

Janey scrunched her eyes shut. "I don't know really. 'Cept…wolves. There's three wolves in the wall…all kind'v dark and scary."

"Hmmm."

Janey waited.

"That might not be such a bad idea. Better than the swimming pool, anyway."

"I never said nothing about a swimming pool!"

The businessman laughed. "No, that's far too mundane for you. I'm surprised you haven't thought to give a free diamond to every person who visits the Castle."

Janey looked at him and stuck out her chin. Mocking a deep voice, she boomed, "Whatta you think, money grows on trees?"

Donald gave her a push toward the schoolhouse, watched her run inside, and turned toward downtown. He had ten more mailings bulging in his briefcase, and he knew the Postmaster liked to have them before 9:00.

The Post Office door crashed against the wall with an explosion of bell-ringing. Donald marched to the window and faced the horrified Postmaster.

"I've got a few more mailings for you this morning, I hope you don't mind."

The Postmaster slowly shook his head. "No, it's not that ..."

"Good. I've got six for Denver, two for the Springs, one for Pueblo, and one for Glenwood. I believe you'll find all the proper postage on them."

"Fine. I don't have a problem with that, it's just..."

Waving goodbye, Donald crashed out the door.

The Postmaster muttered to himself the rest of the morning.

* * *

Ninety feet is a long way to the ground. None of the crew said it, but it had crossed all of their minds. Cracker insisted that only Jake do the finishing work on the turrets, and unfailingly held the ladder for the younger man. He often yelled at Jake to "hurry up" and "take some pride in yer work" to justify his ladder-holding position. But the men knew why he was there.

At this point, much of the crew was dispatched to the inside of the castle, to dig the rink and administer other final touches. Those inside had strict orders not to allow the general public to visit; indeed, no one was supposed to divulge any descriptions of the interior. Cracker knew not every man could hold his tongue at all times, but he also knew that the secrets that slipped out could only tantalize. Rumors circulated around Leadville of ice-fishing ponds and circus arenas inside the Palace. Friends of the workers often chanced by the Castle's gate, bearing excuses and glancing over the men's shoulders. It seemed, at least, that the citizens would pay to visit the palace once.

Donald knew that wasn't enough. And other problems arose.

"Have you seen this?" he asked Sarah, impatiently tapping the newspaper one cold morning in early December.

"No."

"This crackpot Gifford is claiming Leadville will 'rue the day' they voted for the Palace. He says the towers will attract lightning. *Lightning*, for God's sake. He says we'll be lucky if only a few people are killed. What's he going to worry about next—trolls burrowing under the Castle?"

"Trolls don't exist," Janey piped up.

"Shush!" Sarah commanded. She turned toward Donald. "I'm sorry, Mr. Podge. People don't always like to let big things happen. And here in Leadville, well, there's a lot of people left who dreamed of mining the right claim, or dreamed of all the mines and silver putting Leadville on the map right with Denver, and saw the whole thing collapse.

They don't want to see anything collapse again. So they have to expect things to collapse. It's not right, but it happens to people. You just have to prove them wrong…And they want to be proved wrong, that's the crazy thing. You know how that works."

"We'll prove 'em wrong!" Janey cried.

"Shush!" Donald and Sarah turned on her.

* * *

"Ya got that almost finished now, don'tcha Mr. Gunny?" a timid voice asked.

George kept his hose aimed at the wall and looked down at the scraggly eight-year old with big ears.

"Matthew!" he said. "You, you must be icy-cold. Does your m-momma know yer out here?"

The boy smiled softly and shuffled his feet.

* * *

The next morning at the breakfast table, Donald looked over the newspaper at Janey. "You know," he said, "this is probably just a coincidence, but I complained to your mother yesterday about this lightning scare, and here in the paper today there's an anonymous letter explaining that the chances of a lightning strike are remote, and reprimanding the editor for printing irresponsible letters." He glanced at Sarah, who concentrated on tending the coffee.

"Doesn't sound like no coincidence to me," Janey said.

"*A* coincidence. Doesn't sound like *a* coincidence," Sarah corrected.

Donald winked at Janey. "To be honest, it doesn't sound like *a* coincidence to me, either."

* * *

Item, *Leadville Telegraph*, front page: "Tomorrow marks the day all Leadville has been awaiting. Following a parade that commences on Harrison Street and proceeds to the Hill, the Ice Palace will officially open her gates to the public. Fireworks and bands will accompany the ceremonial ribbon-cutting honoring the largest ice castle ever built. Forty cents admission will be charged to adults, and 10 cents to children.

"Immediately following the ribbon-cutting, Mayor Bob Simons will embark on the maiden sled ride in the mile-long bobsled run."

Rumor has it that Johnny Taylor and Scott Myers embarked on the true inaugural run the previous night, well after Gunny and the rest of the town had gone to bed. In the years that followed, countless fathers told their sons the true story: how Johnny and he slipped wildly through the dark on the quiet rush of the fast sled's runners. Somehow, it seemed right that so many people made that first mysterious run.

* * *

Donald stood tall beside his Model T. He wore the same grey suit he had worn the day he had arrived, and what looked to be the same dull tie (it was hard to tell). He held his hat in his hand, and the sun beat down hard upon his forehead. The morning issue of the *Telegraph* had predicted a high of 58 degrees. It was closer to 68.

Most of the town of Leadville stood a respectful distance behind Mayor Bob, who was extending his hand to the businessman.

"Donald Podge," the Mayor boomed in his best

speech-delivering voice, "the city of Leadville is indebted to you for its most memorable winter. Thanks to your efforts, our community has earned itself a place in history: home of the World's Largest Ice Palace!" He glanced down at his notes. "As William Shakespeare, the famous English playwright, once said, 'Some are born great, some achieve greatness, and some have greatness thrust upon them.' Well, it seems almost as if he had Leadville in mind when he wrote those words. This winter, greatness was thrust upon our proud community by Mr. Podge. A great castle made for great fun for our town and indeed, the state of Colorado. To whom do we owe our greatness? A daring businessman from Texas: Donald Podge! [cheers from the crowd] And by the way," the Mayor added in a more confidential tone, "Old Gunny did a pretty fine job himself! [prolonged cheers]."

Mayor Bob shook Donald's hand again and said in a low voice, "Congratulations. To be honest, I wasn't sure you could pull this off."

Donald shrugged. "Not that much to it really. Just took good business sense: recognizing a market, and then creating a demand for a new service. I just had the capital and the know-how, and that's really all you need."

The crowd milled around, uncertain of the next move. A group of twenty or so surrounded Gunny, alternately slapping him on the back and posing loud questions. Sunshine streamed over the landscape, chasing away any lingering resentment toward Leadville's harsh winter climate. For a day, perhaps even a month, no one would ask himself why he built his home at 10,000 feet. The power of the bald, still-white mountains and the sweetness of the air paid the debt in full.

Murmurs crescendoed to muttering as the editor from the *Telegraph* moved out of the crowd and faced Donald.

"How 'bout a quote for posterity?" The newspaperman asked, trying to look congenial.

Donald glared. "Let's just say, some people thought I couldn't make the Palace work, but sound business sense proved them wrong." He paused. "And, oh yeah, put in something about the importance of the support from the town of Leadville."

Gifford retreated extending congratulatory remarks, and Gunny stepped forward. He looked at Donald's hand as he shook it and said simply, "Thanks."

"Thank you," Donald said. "I couldn't have done it without you," he added, suddenly picturing himself holding a fire hose in the dark.

Last to step forward were the Warfields. Sarah glanced at Cracker fumbling for words, and hugged Donald. "It was a good winter," she said.

Cracker pulled himself together and gripped Donald's hand. "You tell all those folks in Texas what a great place Leadville is." He hesitated. "But don't make it sound so great they all come a'runnin' to take over the place. We don't need none of them ten-story buildin's out here." He managed a wink.

Tears held their ground in Janey's eyes. She hugged Donald fiercely and croaked, "Bye."

"Bye, Janey." He moved gently away, waved to the crowd and stepped in his car. The town of Leadville applauded as he drove down the long, sloping road beside the Arkansas River.

* * *

Cracker pried the long nails from the fast-drying lumber. He worked methodically along the south wall of the Castle's reappearing framework. Whenever he freed a beam, he'd call to Jake (the rest of the crew had long since returned to their farms), and they'd move the lumber to the buggy hitched to his horses. Periodically, he'd mumble, "No sense wastin' all this purfec'ly good wood." Jake would quietly nod his assent.

At noon, the men took a break for lunch. Cracker wolfed his sandwich and then wandered around the remains of the castle. When he reached the far northwest corner, he saw a little girl sitting on a rock.

He moved closer and asked, "Young lady, how come you ain't in school?"

Janey turned at the sound of her father's voice. "It's Saturday."

"Oh yeah…" Cracker looked off at the mountains and then back at his daughter. "Sure as Hell…sure was something, weren't it?"

"It was," she said.

He looked away, and then again at her. "Don't stay so long your Mama worries."

"I won't."

Cracker muttered something about Jake loafing and wandered away.

The little girl sat very quietly on her rock, staring vaguely at the castle. The remaining ice sagged heavily on the wood beams, showing patches and holes big enough to walk through. Above, the entire ceiling was bare except for the beams, which framed a fresh blue sky. Birds chirped nearby, and the Leadville Ice Palace echoed them with a steady drip, drip, drip…

THE MASTER'S MANSION

"Thy will be done" were the last words Frederick heard—and then the dreadful white, cruelly bright Being waved His scarred hand.

Frederick half-suspected that his next sight would be fire and brimstone (whatever brimstone might be), but he was pleasantly surprised: he found himself seated in a leather armchair in an enormous hall. He had spent enough time pursuing wealth and comfort to recognize the hall's rich luxury. The paneling, he knew, was mahogany, and the candelabras were 14th century. The furniture, Victorian and ornate, was probably the loveliest he had ever touched; he thrilled as he rested his feet on an intricately-carved ottoman.

"My will being done seems promising," he muttered as he caressed his chin. "Though, of course, part of that would involve port and—" He stopped. Port and cigars lay on the booktable. Before the mirage could vanish, Frederick seized the bottle and splashed the dusty liquid into a crystal tumbler.

He slid the tumbler to his lips and flinched, splashing port on his florid mustache. An oily voice had startled him; it sounded right at his ear, and seemed to have purred, "Welcome to your world."

"What?" Frederick wheeled around, but even as he turned he saw the speaker slide in front of him.

"This is excellent port," the speaker continued, shifting the decanter in his hands. He peered at it through his eyeglasses, which were an odd rust-color. Frederick noticed, in a detached way, that the frames matched the man's pupils.

The man himself was small and lame, and impeccably dressed. The shades of his jacket, his pants and his shirt were muted, but seemed to faintly clash—like most clothes in fashion magazines.

"In fact," the smallish man continued, "port like this has only wetted the lips of a few hundred men in history. And it has graced Waterford crystal like this"—here he snatched the tumbler from Frederick's hand—"in the hands of perhaps a dozen men. It would be a shame to waste it."

The man's upper lip lifted briefly off his teeth, and then he spun and smashed the tumbler in the fireplace.

"What the hell—" Frederick took a step toward the little man.

"Precisely." And with a careless flick of his wrist, he pitched the decanter over his shoulder. It cracked neatly and bloodied the Persian rug below it.

"Good God, you—"

"Yes, but goodness is rather dull, is it not? So many rules," the small man sneered.

The sneer stopped Frederick. He had stepped up with the intention of shaking the lunatic, but the air of ownership in the sneer gave him pause. "Is this your house?" he asked, trying to smuggle a sarcastic tone into the question.

The small man stepped close to him, too close. His breath was a tomb. "Some say," the rusty eyes looked coy, "that this is God's house, since He makes all good things."

"And some say that God is a devil, since the world is so full of evil," Frederick responded automatically. It had been a favorite saying of his for years.

"Hah!" The little man jumped back and clapped. "Well said. Then let's say this is your house—and after all, you know, what's yours is mine." Frederick did not like the way he moved toward the candelabra as he said this.

"Now, just a moment, friend"—Frederick summoned his sternest professorial voice as the fop seized one of the candles—"Just a moment. What's mine may, er I say may be yours, but not yours to destroy. After all …"

"After all, *friend*," the upper lip snapped off the teeth again, "how can it really be mine unless I destroy it?" He walked unhurriedly toward a bookcase.

"Damn it—"

"I shall." The flame of the candle moved dreamily under a first edition of *Paradise Lost*. The book poured oily smoke upward. The small man re-shelved the burning book.

Frederick always prided himself on his assertiveness. Even as his secretary phoned for him and his wife cooked for him and his valet dressed him and his father supported him, he believed he was a "man of action." In keeping with that belief, he leapt into action now, tearing a tapestry from the wall and beating the bookshelf with it.

He stopped suddenly, however, when he realized that the arsonist was helping him. Calmly and coldly, the little man had shed his wool blazer and stood slapping at the fire with it. He registered Frederick's hesitation from the corner of his eye, but continued stoically until the fire was quenched.

"You…are…" Frederick's head was hurting.

The small man stooped to look at the tapestry Frederick still held. As he squinted through his glasses he muttered, "Sixteenth century…quite crumpled and a bit singed…well," he straightened up, "It's a start."

He shook out his blazer, now ragged and sooty. He surveyed the front, and then the back. He wiggled his fingers through a hole in the shoulder. He carefully put the blazer back on.

"You…"

"I say," the small man seemed to have an idea. "You look like a man who can appreciate fine things. I have this beautiful old watch"—gold flashed in his palm as he drew the watch from his pocket—"rubies and everything, you see.

Exquisite craftsmanship. Not another like it in the world, or under it. What do you say? Would you like it?"

The gold glittered in Frederick's eyes. "I would," he breathed quietly, not daring to look at the other man's face.

Snake-like, the palm full of gold glided toward Frederick's own open hand. *Snatch it*, Frederick's brain cried to his hand—but at the same time he heard a sharp hiss and saw the palm turn to a fist. The gold disappeared with a crumple as the small man, supernaturally strong, crushed the watch. In the same motion, he dropped the tangle of parts and broken glass into Frederick's hand. Two small blobs of blood followed, icy cold. Frederick felt sick.

"What's yours is mine, I always say." Turning his back on Frederick, the little man slowly wrapped his hand with a white handkerchief as he limped down the hall. His clip-clop gait matched the ticking of a clock in some far-off room. When he reached the door he turned around. Frederick flinched.

"You are pitifully slow, *friend*." He shook his head. "But you'll learn. You've got plenty of time."

He threw open the door. He took two steps to his right. He jumped through a stained-glass window, and was gone.

THE RESIDUE OF HARD WORK

Fishing is gambling. We understand this when we're young, but we make ourselves forget. At nine years old, there is only one question that matters: "Catch anything?" As adults, we invent priggish slogans: "It's called fishing, not catching." And we forget.

The adrenal glands never forget, though. Put me near a deep trout stream with a disassembled rod, and my veins throb. If I am foolish enough to forego the outhouse before I see the river, I'm usually squatting behind a pine before I tie on a fly, listening to the water roar like the slots in Las Vegas.

Today I remembered the outhouse and also the fly dope, and I'm breathing deeply. I've hired a guide for just the fourth time, and I'm expecting big things. Adults don't fish as often as kids, so when we do we make it a production.

Mike Teague is one hell of a guide, at least according to the adults I know. He doesn't look like much—maybe 5'10" and wiry and hairy. He doesn't wear the traditional bucket hat or even a flyvest, just a grey t-shirt and gorgeous chestwaders and a Budweiser backpack. His attitude bugs me already, but I figure that means he's a good guide. A bad guide can't afford to be a jerk.

Mike scoffs at match-the-hatchers. "Catching trout isn't rocket science," he says. "And trout aren't galloping gourmets. I don't need t' turn over every rock or collect larva samples t' know what a trout's eatin'. Bugs! It's bugs—mostly flyin' bugs. All I need is a Rio Grande King and a Adams—and a Grasshopper for really weird days. That's all anybody who can *fish* needs." He says "fish" the same way one of my old college professors said "think."

You get the feeling you won't live up to it.

"Now are you one of those guys I'm gonna have to hold yer hand?" Mike's squinting at me. You'd think a guide would wear sunglasses.

"I don't think so."

"Well, I do. You look like someone whose mommy fussed a lot over. Ya look like a freakin' Kennedy."

Like an idiot, I begin worrying that I look like a Kennedy.

Mike throws himself down beside me and takes the rod out of my hands. "Oh, this is crap. I guess I'll be usin' this piece today."

"No you won't." I take back my rod. You can do a lot of things to me, but you can't do that. "You don't have to worry about my gear or cleaning my fish. Just tell me what fly you're using and point me in the right direction."

"I'm usin' the Rio Grande. But that doesn't mean you are. Ya fish an Adams—14 'r 16. An' we'll start downstream."

"Downstream?" I try to keep the incredulity out of my voice, but I can't. "I never fish downstream."

Mike draws himself up and squints. "Oh, you never?! Well I guess we can't then. We wouldn't want to change yer ways." He stares.

Mocking doesn't get me, but the stare almost does. Fortunately, I can avert my eyes to clamp my reel on my rod, feed line through, and tie an Adams on my tippet. I am still breathing deeply. My guide is unfriendly, but the weather is perfect—hot for Colorado in June, which is perfect—and the river holds so much promise. I know I'm a pretty good fly fisherman, with or without a guide, and I also know (which is more) that I'll never be great. I lack the precision and the patience to attend to my technique enough to really change it, and my luck is not what it could be. But I know where trout lie in a pool, and I'm not intimidated by the difficulties. A few lucky breaks—especially early in the day—and I could have a big trip. Even without those breaks, I can do enough right to face Mike. I begin to move upstream.

I fish the first likely hole fully conscious of Mike's disapproving stare. "—Almighty!" A curse drifts across the water. "If ya slap the water like that again, ya'll put down every fish in the river." He's exaggerating, but I know what he means. When I rush my cast I pitch the line too hard, and my Adams hits the water too solidly. It's a big problem in slow water, but in this high stream it won't matter much.

Three more casts shut Mike up. They're just what I know them to be: workman-like tosses with decent distance and better accuracy, capably placed to entice trout at the back of the pool first. Mike noisily stomps through willows nearby, and begins fishing the next pool upstream. His casts whirl like a poodle skirt. He seems to care very little about his fly; he looks upstream and up at the sky and at his watch. But when his fly disappears he sets the hook effortlessly, and he hoists a fat rainbow in his net moments later.

"Janny Juny Bunny Boony!" He squints back at me and cackles, holding his catch in the air. "Yer fishin' the wrong fly, Jack!"

I smile grimly and keep fishing. As it happens, I like both the Adams and the Rio Grande King, and I know enough not to abandon a good fly too soon. Mike might be right about my Adams, but I'm hoping he's not right about too much during the day. He's insufferable enough without a good track record.

Mike nets another rainbow before I give up on my first hole, and his grin is wide as I wade through the willows past him. "Boy, ya don't give a good hole much of a chance, do ya?" I don't think he's right about that; I'm too stubborn to quit something too soon. But I'm starting to worry about the Adams.

Three more likely holes without so much as a strike convince me to replace the Adams with the Rio Grande King. To my shame, I crouch behind a boulder to make the switch, hoping that Mike won't notice. I already like him less than anybody I know, and I'm beginning to wonder if my friends have set me up. Can any guide, no matter how skilled, be this annoying?

"Janny Juny Bunny Boony!" I flinch at the same shout I've heard six times in the first hour. What kind of a guide takes pleasure in outfishing you?

The Rio Grande King fares no better than the Adams, and I begin my descent into madness. I begin to talk to the trout, silently, imploring them to honor my ability. "That deserves a strike," I think as I set the Rio Grande King down exactly where it should go, at the top left portion of the circular eddy to the left of the whitewater. "You've got to hit that," I tell the trout telepathically. But the trout remain unimpressed and un- seduced. They love Mike's number 14 Rio Grande King, but my number 14 Rio Grande King might as well be a number 1 Bullfrog in electric pink. I begin to see that the trout are as revolted by my fly as I am by the whole sport of fishing.

"What th' hell is wrong with you?" Mike asks as we sit down to a late lunch of peanut butter sandwiches and warm Budweiser. "Th' fish are practically climbin' outta the river into my net t'day."

"Haven't you ever had bad luck?" I try staring at him. He doesn't notice.

"Yeah. And I've heard of crappy fisherm'n. An' I don't think ya can blame this all on luck."

"I'm fishing the *exact* same fly you are!"

"Yeah, but you ain't fishin' the same. I don't beat the water like I'm whippin' a horse in the stretch, an' I don't yank my fly out the second it sets down. Yer doin' all ya can to spook those—"

"Shut up." The words are out of my mouth before I think. Mike's eyes get wide and mean at the same time.

"Shut up?! You little..." He clamps his mouth shut. "Yer lucky I don't kick yer ass right now. If you weren't..."

I stand up. "Let's go." My fists are clenched, and I don't mean "Let's leave." I want to fight, but the angrier I get the less articulate I am.

Mike knows what I mean. He puts a hand down to push himself up, but he pauses while he's still crouched.

"Ah, screw it," he says, and he sits back down.

I am suddenly embarrassed. What I did wasn't right. I know I should apologize, but I can't. And I don't feel like sitting down again.

"Listen," Mike says. "I've got my limit, so I can help ya more this aft'rnoon. If ya still wanna fight after we're done, I'm ready. But I think y'll be feelin' better t'night." He drains his Budweiser and throws it in the willows. I pick it up, put it in my pack, and mutter, "Okay."

The afternoon is much, much worse. I never like advice, and I hate it much more when it comes from Mike. According to him, everything I do is wrong, even when I do just what he demands. Switching to a smaller Rio Grande King doesn't work, nor does the Grasshopper. Using a rollcast doesn't work, allowing an exaggerated drift doesn't work, eschewing the fly dope doesn't work, and tying on a lighter tippet doesn't work. Ignoring all Mike says and fishing according to my strengths doesn't work. At one point, Mike actually maps out every cast for me, and I hit every spot in the hole in the order he dictates. Doesn't work.

Still, Mike knows that it's somehow my fault. After I abandon the hole that skunked me in spite of obeying Mike's directions, he casts twice to the same places and—"Janny Juny

Bunny Boony!"—hauls out a big brown. "See what I'm talkin'
'bout?" he asks.

I try not to talk. When things get really ugly I take a
big breath and look up at the valley. *How can anyone be angry
on a day like this?* I ask myself. I catalog the blue of the sky,
the smell of the air, the sun on the river, the aspens, and my
health. And I am still so angry I could hold Mike's head
underwater.

It's hard to fit luck into a universe ruled by the God of
the Bible. Free will fits pretty easily, I think, even when one
acknowledges that God foreknows everything and is bringing
history to its appointed end. But luck? Luck presupposes a
chaotic realm, where rewards and punishments are handed out
without regard to what anyone deserves or needs. Luck
certainly isn't just, and it isn't gracious either. Grace requires a
giver, and luck demands a void so arbitrary that no purposeful
giver can exist.

So I know that I should not view this day as bad luck. I
should see instead Providence, pre-ordaining a scenario to
help me grow and conform to the image of Christ. I *should* see
this, but I can't. Fishing is not entirely luck, and I'm too good
a fisherman to be embarrassed this badly.

But the day does, in fact, end with me badly
embarrassed. The scoreboard looks good—Mike has his limit
and I have my limit—but the truth is, Mike caught and kept
twice his limit and hung half of them on my stringer. I suspect
he is particularly pleased that he thought of this new
humiliation for me.

I made up my mind that I would not fight Mike, but the
hike back to his truck makes keeping my commitment
difficult. Mike is obnoxious in a way almost unheard of in
outdoorsmen—he doesn't know when to shut up. I give him
every sign that I have heard enough, and he talks and talks, as
though his voice is the song of a siren. He seems to fall under

his own spell, charmed into loquaciousness.

When we reach his truck, I know what I have to do. As Mike climbs into the cab, I climb into the back of the truck.

"What th' hell..."

"I need the fresh air," I say, and I stare at the first star over the forest.

In this way I succeed at one thing: I don't fight Mike. Jesus makes it clear in His Sermon on the Mount, however, that I am still guilty of murder in my heart.

Knowing all this, you will probably be surprised to hear that I hired Mike to guide me three more times in the next three years. If it sounds perverse, I can assure you that it felt perverse at the time as well. What kind of a man hires a guide that abuses and despises him, never helping him catch a trout? I can't say. My only defense is this: men who lose their life savings in a casino will freely walk back into that casino with their savings again. And I am only fishing, after all.

Perhaps you will not be so surprised to hear that in these next three trips with Mike, I never see so much as a strike, while Mike fills both our limits each time. Like any superstitious man, I manipulated every variable: upstream, downstream, night fishing, flies as mundane as the Black Ant and as exotic as the Silver Doctor, floating leaders and sinking leaders, Zebco rods and bamboo heirlooms, tiny mountain creeks and wide lazy oxbows, even—dare I say it?—an Adams secretly drenched in Power Bait. Nothing works. More accurately, everything fails.

Mike grows more obnoxious with each trip. We have not mentioned fighting again, but we think about it all the time. The difference is that I grow more tight-lipped while Mike, if possible, grows more talkative. Each hour I spend with him I promise myself that it will be the last hour I ever have to hear the sound of his voice. Each trip back to town ends with me freezing, huddled in the bed of his truck.

All of which may or may not explain how we got here. Today, I hire Mike for the fifth time. There is no doubt this time will be the last—not because I have learned will-power, but simply because Mike moves to Korea tomorrow. He assures me that the woman with whom he is moving in is "totally hot and knows her place." I try to tell him I am sorry to see him go. I am a very bad liar.

This day I have dared to do what very few gamblers dare: I have rigged the deck. Today the house hands loaded dice to the man who brought them and knows how to use them. Today Mike is "guiding" me on the South Platte, specifically on a remote stretch I have fished since childhood. Not only has this river never let me down; more than once it has restored my confidence after a hellish day with Mike. I cannot wait to scream "Janny Juny Bunny Boony" as I wave my first trout at him.

At least, that's how things should have worked. Instead, unbelievably and inexorably, Mike's wicked magic poisons my favorite stream. A casual observer might mildly conclude that only one thing happens—a talky fisherman catches some fish while a tense fisherman catches none. But you know better. You can see what I saw: the darkest entity killing me for the sake of killing.

On the hike back to the truck I store every obnoxious word as a precious marker guaranteeing my right to fight Mike. It no longer matters to me that I haven't fought anyone since fourth grade, or that Mike fights in bars all the time. All that matters is that my first punch to that hairy chin will close his mouth.

The cold rain that starts to fall strengthens my resolve. A fight in warm sunshine might feel strange. This will only feel good.

"Listen, man, I've got a fav'r t' ask."

We are within sight of Mike's truck, and I don't like

the insinuating tone in his voice. "What?"

"Ya know how ya always ride in th' bed?"

I nod.

"Well—I still ain't outta my apartment, so I don't really have time t' drive ya inta town. Can y' just hitch a ride in the back of some oth'r truck?"

I nod. "No problem."

Mike sticks out his hairy hand, and I shake it. "Thanks, man." He looks over my shoulder.

"No problem." I wave as he drives away.

EULOGY

"Please forgive me for reading…I'm not used to speaking in public. I wrote down what I wanted to say because I wasn't sure that I could never…I mean ever, get it right.

"Uh…Before I read it, though, I just wanted to say that I knew there would be this many people here—I mean, I knew a lot of people loved Jay. And I'm glad you came, and I know he's looking down…and he *is*, too. And I wanted to say, too, how sorry I am, Mrs. Croel, that those funeral people lost his body, but, you know, the body isn't really the important thing; it's just that, he's still with us in our hearts. Anyway …

"Ahem. I never thought I'd be doing this. Jay and I joked about who would go first and I always told him that he'd better will his Babe Ruth autographed ball to me when he died, but that's not what I mean. In the first place, neither one of us ever thought we would go so soon. But more than that, I never thought I'd be doing this because for the past few months I've been so angry with Jay that I didn't think I'd care if he died. I know most of you know that, and I hope those that didn't will still listen.

"Let me say at the start: Jay was the best friend I ever had. He moved next door when we were six, and we were playing Batman and Robin before they unloaded the truck. When I learned to swim, he had to learn how to swim, and when anyone bullied him I punched them in the nose. I looked out for him, and as much as he could he looked out for me.

"Most friends drift apart as they go off to school and start their careers, but Jay and I wouldn't let that happen. Thanks to alphabetical seating we sat next to each other all through grade school; some teachers even called us 'C' and 'C minor.' In high school I captained the football team and Jay backed me up, and we double-dated and skipped class and did everything together. When it came time to choose a college, it made sense to choose the same one: if Colorado State wanted one of us, they'd have to take us both.

"That's what I'm trying to say: we were peas in a pod. We liked the same things, but we also thought the same things. Some of you probably know that feeling, where it really seems like you can read another person's mind. Identical twins separated at birth, that's what we were—except we didn't look identical. But there were days when we'd just show up at the same fishing hole at the same time, or blurt out the same thing, or catch each other's eye and just *know* what the other was thinking.

"Lots of people bugged me about why I always hung out with Jay. He wasn't cool enough, they'd say, or he was a troublemaker, but I didn't care. We were inseparable.

"Some people said—when Jay was alive but they wouldn't say it now—that he acted holier-than-thou. I think there's some truth in that, but in a good way. Jay never *said* anything to make you think he was better than you, but he always avoided doing the marginal things—the stuff you felt guilty about while you were doing it. And sometimes he did things I didn't want to do but felt like maybe I should. What I mean is, Jay *did* act better than the rest of us, but not out of pride or to be a teacher's pet. He just was better.

"At least, I thought that way until he stole Sarah. You may not know this, but I dated—I loved—Sarah before they got married. Jay liked to say that I introduced them, but I did more than that: I fell for Sarah head over heels, and I took her everywhere with Jay and me. And while I blindly waltzed along, Jay stole her.

"It was funny, because at first he didn't even seem to like her. I remember, he told me once that she was too controlling, and a lot of times he begged me to break up with her. When he said that, I thought it was because he was jealous, but later I saw it was because he wanted her himself.

"A lot of times I thought Jay was rude to Sarah. She would try to say something nice to him, and he would just turn his head. But in a weird way I think that caused all the trouble, because Sarah couldn't stand to have anyone dislike her, and so she began to work really hard to make Jay notice her and talk to her.

"And then one day, Jay's attitude changed. He noticed Sarah, all right, and before I knew it he was charming her. Great! I thought. Now my best friend and my future wife can be best friends, too. Some people warned me that Jay was stealing my girl, but I was the football star, and besides, best friends don't do that.

"Well, you know I was wrong. Jay—Jay!—broke the news to me—not Sarah. And all he did was look sad and say, 'You may not know this, Pete, but Sarah's in love with me and we're engaged. I hope you can forgive me.'

"Forgive! What I wanted to do was punch him. But I was too stunned to do anything but stare. How could he? How could my best friend *betray* me, and then just…look at me as calm as a cow? How *could* he?

"Excuse me…I'm sorry…Sorry. It's hard for me to talk about this. I know you don't want to hear about me, but I'm trying to explain about Jay…

"Anyway, most of you saw their wedding—I didn't. I was furious. He asked me to be the best man, of course, but I told him that I hated him and that he didn't deserve a best man. You have to understand, I reacted so strongly because Jay had been *such* a good friend. If he was just your typical guy I wouldn't have been so shocked by his betrayal. But his loyalty and…*goodness* made it so hard to take.

"And then he died—just like that. One day they're on their way to the honeymoon, and the next day he's gone. But before he died something else happened.

"The morning after the wedding, I got a package in the mail. I could tell it was Jay's handwriting, and at first I didn't want to open it, but I was curious. When I did open it, I couldn't believe it: the pearl of great price! At least, that's what we always called his Babe Ruth ball. And there it was: he had shipped it to me like it was nothing at all.

"Well, you can imagine how I felt about that. Sure, I wanted the baseball, but who did he think I was? Did he think he could just *buy* my friendship back? Like some *thing* could replace Sarah in my life? In some ways, that was the worst insult of all. How dare he think of me that way?

"You can bet I kept the baseball, but I didn't forgive him. I decided then and there that I'd been wrong about him all along, and that I'd always hate him. When I heard about his death I knew exactly how I wanted to feel: vindicated and happy. But in spite of myself I started to cry ...

"And that's what I'm trying to say. I thought I'd be happy to hear that Jay was dead, to know that he got what I thought he deserved. And instead—I was so mad about this— instead I kept feeling sadder and sadder. I cried when I heard and I cried when I thought about it. And then I had a weird thought: I wasn't sad because I felt guilty or because I was on some kind of emotional roller coaster—I was sad because I didn't spend the last few months of Jay's life being his best friend! I was sad because I was going to miss him, terribly.

"Sorry...

"Okay, that's the end of the speech but it's not quite all I want to say. I know I'm not supposed to say this, because it's not sensitive to Sarah's parents and all, but listen: Sarah's wanted. Jay died in a suspicious way, and Sarah disappeared in a suspicious way. And now when I hold that baseball I

wonder, you know, did he send it to me because he...*could*
he...

"Okay, Mrs. Croel, I'm done. I'm done. I'm sorry I
didn't say that better. But what I wanted to say was this: I
didn't deserve Jay as a friend. Not when we were six, and not
when he stole Sarah. Jay was better than me and he was better
than any of you. Maybe I'm wrong, but even his betrayal
doesn't feel like it should ..."

ENDNOTES

[1] T.S. Eliot, "The Idea of a Christian Society," *Christianity and Culture* (San Diego, CA: Harcourt Brace & Co., 1976), p. 32.

[2] I am not arguing here that the *content* of these works is Christian; I am merely pointing out that the *form* of each of these books is beautiful.

[3] John William Ward, "Afterword" in Harriet Beecher Stowe, *Uncle Tom's Cabin* (New York, NY: Signet, 1981), p. 480.

[4] See Dorothy Sayers, "The Dogma is the Drama," *The Whimsical Christian* (New York, NY: Macmillan Publishing Co., 1987).

[5] Gene Edward Veith, *Reading Between the Lines* (Wheaton, IL: Crossway, 1990), p. 46.

[6] C.S. Lewis expounds on this in *Mere Christianity* (New York, NY: Macmillan, 1960).

[7] Louis Whitworth, *Literature Under the Microscope: A Christian Case for Reading* (Richardson, TX: Probe Publications, 1984), p.14.

[8] Edith Wharton, *Ethan Frome* (New York, NY: Charles Scribner's Sons, 1939), p. 85.

[9] Notice that I am not referring to satire here. Writers of satire will often ironically elevate the trivial or denigrate the profound, because they trust their readers to recognize the inversion. Satire only works if the reader understands the absurdity of the perspective argued by the satirist.

[10] Ernest Hemingway, cited in Jon Winokur, ed., *Writers on Writing* (Philadelphia, PA: Running Press, 1986), p. 55.

[11] F. Scott Fitzgerald, cited in Sheilah Graham and Gerold Frank, *Beloved Infidel* (New York, NY: Henry Holt and Co., 1958), p. 215.

[12] Mark Twain, *Pudd'nhead Wilson* (New York, NY: Signet Classics, 1964), p. 79.

[13] In fairness to Kafka, it's possible that this is the fault of his worldview rather than his prose. How much information can a man provide, if his whole view of life is negation and emptiness?

[14] Charles Dickens, *A Christmas Carol* (New York, NY: Scholastic, 1999), pp. 15-16.

[15] Alexander Solzhenitsyn, *One Day in the Life of Ivan Denisovich* (New York, NY: Signet, 1963), p. 158.

[16] Truman Capote, cited in Winokur, *Writers on Writing*, p. 113.

[17] John Steinbeck, *The Long Valley* (New York, NY: Penguin Books, 1986), p. 34.

[18] C.S. Lewis, *On Stories, and Other Essays on Literature* (New York, NY: Harcourt Brace Jovanovich, 1982), p. 16.

[19] Francis Bacon, "Of Studies," *The Essays* (New York, NY: Penguin Books, 1985), p. 209.

[20] Lewis, *On Stories, and Other Essays on Literature*, p. 35.

[21] E.B. White and William Strunk, *The Elements of Style* (Boston, MA: Allyn and Bacon, 2000), p. 84.

[22] Of course we're only discussing fiction writing here. While some of the Twelve Trademarks apply to both fiction and non-fiction, some are the exclusive property of fiction. In a sense, this trademark points out the main distinction between fiction and non-fiction: non-fiction *tells* and fiction *shows*. I think this is the reason why fiction is more persuasive than non-fiction and why literature is ultimately more important than philosophy. People are seldom persuaded by a syllogism—but the right story can change a man's whole perspective.

[23] F. Scott Fitzgerald, *The Last Tycoon* (New York, NY: Charles Scribner's Sons, 1941), p. 163.

[24] See William Kilpatrick, *Why Johnny Can't Tell Right from Wrong* (New York, NY: Simon & Schuster, 1992).

[25] Harold Bloom, *The Western Canon* (New York, NY: Riverhead Books, 1995), p. 3.

[26] Thomas Carlyle, *Heroes and Hero-Worship* (Boston, MA: Dana Estes and Co.), p. 351.

[27] I think God provides important "hints" about literary skill in the Bible, as I've indicated throughout this essay. Certainly literary skill requires a reliance on our God-given conscience and an understanding that we know

a man by his fruit. In addition, we can see literary skill modeled for us in scripture, especially in Job and certain Psalms.

[28] T.S. Eliot, cited in George Plimpton, ed., *Writers at Work: Second Series* (New York, NY: Penguin Books, 1977), p. 102.

[29] At least, great authors always have the last eleven trademarks in view. Non-Christian authors may only sub-consciously realize that the dogma is the drama.

[30] Though not, I would argue, trademarks number 1, 7, 8, 10, 11, or 12. These trademarks are essential components of a great story.

[31] Blaise Pascal, *Pensees* (New York, NY: Penguin, 1986), p. 245.

[32] Ibid., p. 42.

[33] Ibid., p. 154.

[34] V.I. Lenin, *The State and Revolution* (New York, NY: International, 1932), pp. 73-4.

[35] B.F. Skinner, *Walden Two* (New York, NY: Macmillan, 1962).

[36] Hammudah Abdalati, *Islam in Focus* (Indianapolis, IN: American Trust, 1977), p. 32.

[37] M. Russell Ballard, *Our Search for Happiness* (Salt Lake City, UT: Deseret, 1993), p. 87.

[38] David J. Wolpe, *Teaching Your Children About God* (New York, NY: Henry Holt & Co., 1993), p. 137.

[39] Pascal, *Pensees*, p. 87.

[40] T.H. Huxley, "Naturalism and Supernaturalism," *Agnosticism and Christianity, and Other Essays* (Buffalo, NY: Prometheus Books, 1992), p. 115.

[41] Julian Huxley, in an interview Nov. 21, 1959, cited in Sol Tax, *Evolution of Life* (Chicago, IL: University of Chicago Press, 1960), p. 1.

[42] Aldous Huxley, *The Perennial Philosophy* (New York, NY: Harper & Row, 1970), p. 14.

[43] Aldous Huxley, cited in Robert S. Baker, *Brave New World: History, Science, and Dystopia* (Boston, MA: Twayne Publishers, 1990), p. 5.

[44] Bram Stoker, *Dracula* (New York, NY: Bantam Books, 1989), p. 200.

[45] This metaphysical position is usually described as naturalism. Atheists, in an effort to be consistent, usually rely on a naturalistic philosophy.

[46] Phillip Johnson, *Reason in the Balance* (Downers Grove, IL: InterVarsity Press, 1995), pp. 7-8.

[47] Ibid., p. 14.

[48] Christians interested in organizations focused on the creation/evolution debate would do well to contact the Institute for Creation Research, P.O. Box 2662, El Cajon, CA 92021 or Answers in Genesis, P.O. Box 6330, Florence, KY 41022.

[49] C.S. Lewis, *The Case for Christianity* (New York, NY: Macmillan, 1989), p. 32.

[50] Herman Melville in a letter to Nathaniel Hawthorne, Julian Hawthorne, *Nathaniel Hawthorne and his Wife* (Boston, MA: Osgood, 1885), vol. 1, p. 401.

[51] Melville in a letter to Hawthorne, Willard Thorp, ed., *Herman Melville: Representative Selections* (New York, NY: American Book Co., 1938), p. 394.

[52] This excellent book is out of print. It was published by Princeton University Press in 1952.

[53] Herman Melville, *Billy Budd, Sailor* (New York, NY: Penguin, 1985), pp. 400-401.

[54] Thompson, *Melville's Quarrel with God*, p. 423.

[55] Melville, *Billy Budd, Sailor*, p. 323.

[56] Ibid., pp. 328-330.

[57] Ibid., pp. 330-331.

[58] Ibid., p. 356.

[59] Ibid., p. 394.

[60] Ibid., pp. 331-332.

[61] Ibid., p. 378.

[62] Ibid., p. 385.

[63] Harold Beaver, "Notes," *Billy Budd, Sailor*, p. 462.

[64] Bertrand Russell, *Human Society in Ethics and Politics* (New York, NY: Mentor, 1962), p. viii.

[65] C.S. Lewis, *God in the Dock* (Grand Rapids, MI: Eerdmans, 1972), p. 294.